Hebrew Bible

Book of

Deuteronomy

Five books of Moses

SimchatChaim.com

There is no known book without mistakes. Therefore, I ask in every language of application if anyone has any questions, comments, clarifications, corrections, please send to: simchatchaim@yahoo.com

All material used in this section may not be used for commercial purposes, but only for study and teaching.

To get this book or books and information Email me at:

simchatchaim@yahoo.com

מהדורה שניה תשפ"ד
Second edition 2024

The contents of the book

Introduction to the

Jewish Bible

First you need to know that the Bible was originally written in the holy language, which today is called Hebrew.

The Tanach itself went through a series of translations from language to language until today's English language.

As a whole, the Tanakh was translated from the holy language into Greek, and from Greek into Latin, and from there into the ancient Agalic, and then into the more modern English.

The problem is when translating from language to language the original meaning is lost.

In the translation of languages there is no realistic possibility to make a completely accurate translation, since in every language there are several translation options for most words, and each word has a different connotation, and also differs to a certain extent from the exact connotation of the original word in the source language.

For example, it is possible to translate the word - שמים. **sky** into English for Sky and Heaven. Two suitable options that each have a different meaning from the other, and also slightly different from the full connotation of the word **sky שמים**. For this reason, along with the attempt to bridge the cultural difference, every translation is actually also an interpretation. In many cases, the translators took the approach of **extensive translation**, in which the translation adds details and interpretations beyond the original text, changes the content, and describes what is happening in a way that is more suitable to the cultural concepts accepted for the period and region. In the common translations these changes are found - to a certain degree of change - in tens of percent of the verses. The general public in these periods knew the Bible only from the translations, and therefore in different regions they actually knew different versions of the same texts, according to the local halachic belief.

The most classic example of this is this:
In the book of Exodus chapter 34 verse 29 it is explained that - KARAN [קרן] the skin of Moses face.

The word KARAN [קרן] has at least two meanings:
A. Radiant.
B. A horn, like that of a bull.
There are other meanings to this word that do not belong to this introduction.

An incorrect translation of the Book of Exodus by Jerome [the Vulgate] into Latin led to an error in the interpretation of the phrase - The horn of the skin of his face. [Exodus 34:29]. And because of this, in

Renaissance sculptures, Mose 's forehead was added **Horns**.

And this is the verse in its entirety according to our translation [compare it to your Bible] - So Moses came down from Mount Sinai. And as Moses came down from the mountain bearing the two tablets of the Pact, Moses was not aware that the skin of his face was **radiant**, since he had spoken with God.

It is known that Hebrew has a vowel for every word. And there can be a word that has a different vowel from the same word. For example, the word with four letters - מ.ד.ב.ר

מְדַבֵּר - speaker.

מִדְבָּר - desert.

מַדְבֵּר - A speaking man.

מִדְבָר - out of nothing.

מְדֻבָּר - thing that is being discussed.

There are **only** five vowels with the same word, and really this word has 25 vowel types!!!! which can change the entire meaning of the verse and the translation.

The first translations of the Bible were created by Jews at the beginning of the first millennium AD. During this period, most Jews gradually stopped using the Hebrew language, especially biblical Hebrew. A translated Bible became a basic necessity for the reading of the Torah in the synagogues, which was performed by two people - one who read the verse is in the original language, and an interpreter repeats his words in the spoken language.

The first translations of the Bible were created by Jews at the beginning of the first millennium AD. During this period, most Jews gradually stopped using the Hebrew language, especially biblical Hebrew. A translated Bible became a basic necessity for the reading of the Torah in the synagogues, which was performed by two people - one who read the verse is in the original language, and an interpreter repeats his words in the spoken language.

The Bible translations can be divided into two main types - Jewish translations and Christian translations. There are a number of differences between the two, the most prominent of which is the inclusion of the New Testament in Christian translations as opposed to its absence in Jewish translations. The Jewish translations were made mainly from the original Hebrew text, and most of the early Jewish translations were made only into separate parts of the Bible, with the intention that they will be used as a commentary on the Bible. In contrast, the Christian translations are mostly intended for independent use, and most of them are based on the Greek translation translated into Latin - the Latin Vulgate.

The truth is that the Holy Scriptures should not be translated into any language. But because of an act explained in the Talmud there was no choice and the Jews translated it.

And the story is:
And this was due to the incident of King Ptolemy, as it is taught in a Baraita: There was an incident involving King Ptolemy of Egypt, who assembled seventy-two Elders from the Sages of Israel, and put them into seventy-two separate rooms, and did not reveal to them for what purpose he assembled them, so that they would not coordinate their responses. He entered and approached each and every one, and said to each of them: Write for me a translation of the Torah of Moses your teacher. The Holy One, Blessed be He, placed wisdom in the heart of each and every one, and they all agreed to one common understanding. Not only did they all translate the text correctly, they all introduced the same changes into the translated text.

And the Talmud [Megillah 9a] continues to say that all 72 sages did not translate it exactly, but changed several verses, for example:

And they wrote for him: God created in the beginning [**Bereshit**], reversing the order of the words in the first phrase in the Torah that could be misinterpreted as: **Bereshit created God** [Genesis 1:1]. Instead of: Come, let us go down, and there confound their language [Genesis 11:7], which indicates multiple authorities, they wrote in the singular: Come, let me go down, and there confound their language. In addition, they replaced the verse: "And Sarah laughed within herself [**bekirba**] [Genesis 18:12], with: And Sarah laughed among her relatives [**bikroveha**].

They made this change to distinguish between Sarah's laughter, which God criticized, and Abraham's laughter, to which no reaction is recorded. Based on the change, Sarah's laughter was offensive because she voiced it to others….

The church father Hieronymus [about 325-420], who knew Hebrew in addition to Latin and Greek, and specialized in theology, created an improved homogenous translation from all the Latin translations. In his work, which was done between the years 390-405, he was greatly assisted by the Jews he knew. The translation of the first books he dealt with [first prophets, Samuel and kings] was done closely to the Hebrew text, but the last books [Joshua, Judges, Ruth and Esther] were translated by him in a freer manner. In any case, Hieronymus relied on the Hebrew version, because he noticed the deviations that the Greek translations have from the Hebrew original.

The Vulgate was recognized by the Church in 1546 as the authoritative text of the Holy Scriptures. It includes, apart from the books of the Bible and the New Testament, also the translation of the external books. The name **Vulgate** [=Common] can be translated by Roger Bacon, and when the internal division into chapters was made in the Vulgate.

The English translation - a translation of parts of the Bible into English was made starting from the 7th century. A complete translation of the Bible into English, made under the direction of John Wycliffe, from the Latin version of the Vulgate, was published in about 1380. The church condemned this translation, because it saw the interpretation that accompanied it as heretical. Further English translations were also rejected by the church and the king.

In 1530 William Tyndale translated only the Pentateuch from the Greek in the Kaspela edition into English, and 5 years later Miles Coverdale published the entire Bible in English. James I, King of England initiated the creation of an official translation of the Bible and the New Testament into English. His initiative came against the background of the bitter struggle between Protestants and Catholics in England and Scotland. King James proposed to write a new English translation that would be acceptable to Protestants and Catholics alike. This translation, made from Hebrew and Greek, was published in 1611, and is called the "King James Version, KJV". This translation is still considered the authorized translation of the English Bible [Authorized Version]; Researchers from the universities of London, Oxford and Cambridge worked on it. They also used a Jewish commentary for the translation. In this edition, King James demanded to cleanse the kings of any evil that could cling to them, in order to purify the institution of the monarchy. In the translation, an effort was made to maintain the structure of the Hebrew text, and to convert as much as possible a Hebrew word into an English word. However, a Hebrew word may be translated into different words in English in different contexts, this is to keep the language fluid. The attempt to literally translate Hebrew idioms created new expressions in English, which gradually became part of the English language and culture.

The book of Deuteronomy

The Book of Deuteronomy or **Chumash Devarim** is the fifth Pentateuch among the five books of the Torah, the Pentateuch is also called **Mishna Torah**.

In the book of Numbers, Moses with the children of Israel went in the desert on the way to the Holyland. They faced challenges upon entering the land, and many more new commandments. These words are spoken on the plains of Moab, this was their last stop in the desert, in the fortieth year after the exodus from Egypt, from the 1st of Shevat until the death of Moses on the 7th of Adar [From February till March].

Like the other volumes of the Pentateuch, the book of Deuteronomy bears a name based on the first significant word that appears in the first chapter - **These are the things** (Deuteronomy, 1:1). Its ancient name, from the time of the Sages was - **Mishna Torah**, according to what is written in it - **And he wrote this Mishna Torah for him** (Deuteronomy 17, 18). It is because it is a summary of what was said in the previous four books.

A similar tradition is called the book **Δευτερονόμιον** in the Greek Septuagint translation or **Deuteronomium** in the Latin Vulgate translation, meaning **second law**, or a direct translation of the phrase - **Mishna Torah** as understood by the Greek translators.

The core of the book of Deuteronomy is the speech of Moses in which he reviews the history of the people of Israel and the laws he received. To a large extent, the book of Deuteronomy repeats many details that have already been described in the other books of the Torah, but it does so in a unique style, by changing details and emphasizing matters such as the issue of concentrating on worship - **In a place of happiness that God will choose**, or the prohibition of offering sacrifices outside the Temple, which was presented in the style another in the book of Leviticus, chapter 17.

The style of the book of Deuteronomy is different from that of the other books of the Torah: most of it consists of a speeches that Moses gave to the Israelites on the plains of Moab, before they entered the land of Canaan - aka the Land of Israel. There are two poetry chapters in the book, chapters 12 and 13. The sentences in the book are slightly longer and more complex than normal Hebrew, and he uses a language relatively full of rhetorical allusions - such as **great cities and shapes in the sky** and the like.

The speech of Moses, which is the core of the book of Deuteronomy, talks about God, who chose the people of Israel to be His people because of His love and commitment to the three fathers [Abraham, Issac, and Jacob]. The people of Israel are obligated to fulfill the mitzvot that God commanded them - this is how the book opens, and this is how it closes. The last chapter - chapter 34 - talks about the death of Moses.

The first part - **These are the things that Moses spoke about** (Deuteronomy, 1, 1), also mentions the opening of the Pentateuch - **And these are the names of the children of Israel**, including moral preaching to the people and his proof of sins in the desert. Moses rebuke (Chapters 1 - 4) A non-chronological historical review and a historiosophical and theosophical analysis of various events that happened to the Israelites in the desert, beginning with God's commandment for their journey from **Horeb** after the giving of the Torah, through the location of Mount Sinai itself, and ending with the preaching of morality and a warning about idolatry and its consequences, and with the promise or Demand for repentance. Then there is a pause in the speech, and it is told about the practical existence of the mitzvah of separating cities of refuge, in the past of the eastern Jordan by Moses.

The second part - **And Moses called to all Israel**, also reminds of the opening of the Pentateuch - **And God called to Moses**, is the mitzvot part, in which a large part of the Torah commandments is reproduced, sometimes with the addition of a reason and explanation. Moses repeats the Ten Commandments, commands the uniqueness of the Name, and continues with a series of commands, warnings and moral preachings for the arrival of Israel in their new land.

After that he returned to his historical review and reviews the golden calf incident, and returns to his long sermon.

In the third part - **These are the laws and the judgments that you shall observe to do in the land**, (Deuteronomy, 12, 1). Moses commands mainly all the laws and commandments that are intrinsically related to the Land of Israel. The laws teach how one should behave and not serve foreign Gods, in the land of Israel, and adds details in many commandments, Like the sacrifices, how to distinguish between true prophets and false prophets, mitzvot related to the legal system in Israel, the mitzvot of three legs (chapters 12-16), the laws of Sage that preached against what Moses taught. And the laws of kings and laws of war, and many other laws (chapters 17-20). At the beginning of the third part Moses commands the observance of **Mount Gerizim** and **Mount Aibal** where the people of Israel will make a covenant with God to observe all the commandments of the Torah, and in particular the commandments listed in this part of the book of Deuteronomy, where commandments concerning Israel's settlement in the land appear.

The fourth part - **And Moses spoke to all Israel** (Deuteronomy, 27:9), also reminds us of the opening of the Pentateuch in the desert - **And the Lord spoke to Moses**, opens with another commandment to establish the location of **Mount Gerizim** and **Mount Ibal** where the people of Israel will make a covenant With God on the commandments of the book of Deuteronomy. After that, Moses enumerates a series of blessings that Israel will receive if they keep these commandments, and a series of curses if they break the covenant and do not keep these commandments. Moses adds many threats and warnings about the punishments expected for those who break the covenant (chapters 27 - l), which reach their climax in the song of listening (Deuteronomy, 32).

In this way Moses actually **wraps up** the commandments of the land listed in the third part of the book, with the command to make the covenant on **Mount Gerizim** and **Mount Aibal**, which appears before these commandments (Deuteronomy, 11:20 6-32), and immediately after them (Deuteronomy 27).

The fifth part is the end of the book and the entire Torah. Moses bid farewell to the people of Israel with general and personal blessings for each tribe (Deuteronomy, 33), ascends to the top of the peak and looks at the promised land, which he was not allowed to enter.

Deuteronomy

Devarim

Chapter 1

1. These are the words which Moses spoke unto all Israel beyond the Jordan; in the wilderness, in the Arabah, over against Suph, between Paran and Tophel, and Laban, and Hazeroth, and Di-zahab.

2. It is eleven days journey from Horeb unto Kadesh-barnea by the way of mount Seir.

3. And it came to pass in the fortieth year, in the eleventh month, on the first day of the month, that Moses spoke unto the children of Israel, according unto all that the LORD had given him in commandment unto them;

4. After he had smitten Sihon the king of the Amorites, who dwelt in Heshbon, and Og the king of Bashan, who dwelt in Ashtaroth, at Edrei;

5. Beyond the Jordan, in the land of Moab, took Moses upon him to expound this law, saying:

6. The LORD our God spoke unto us in Horeb, saying: Ye have dwelt long enough in this mountain;

7. Turn you, and take your journey, and go to the hill-country of the Amorites and unto all the places nigh thereunto, in the Arabah, in the hill-country, and in the Lowland, and in the South, and by the sea-shore;

The land of the Canaanites, and Lebanon, as far as the great river, the river Euphrates.

8. Behold, I have set the land before you: go in and possess the land which the LORD swore unto your fathers, to Abraham, to Isaac, and to Jacob, to give unto them and to their seed after them.

9. And I spoke unto you at that time, saying: I am not able to bear you myself alone;

10. The LORD your God hath multiplied you, and, behold, ye are this day as the stars of heaven for multitude.

11. The LORD, the God of your fathers, make you a thousand times so many more as ye are, and bless you, as He hath promised you!

12. How can I myself alone bear your cumbrance, and your burden, and your strife?

13. Get you, from each one of your tribes, wise men, and understanding, and full of knowledge, and I will make them heads over you.

14. And ye answered me, and said: The thing which thou hast spoken is good for us to do.

15. So, I took the heads of your tribes, wise men, and full of knowledge, and made them heads over you, captains of thousands, and captains of hundreds, and captains of fifties, and captains of tens, and officers, tribe by tribe.

16. And I charged your judges at that time, saying: Hear the causes between your brethren, and judge righteously between a man and his brother, and the stranger that is with him.

17. Ye shall not respect persons in judgment; ye shall hear the small and the great alike; ye shall not be afraid of the face of any man; for the judgment is God's; and the cause that is too hard for you ye shall bring unto me, and I will hear it.

18. And I commanded you at that time all the things which ye should do.

19. And we journeyed from Horeb, and went through all that great and dreadful wilderness which ye saw, by the way to the hill-country of the Amorites, as the LORD our God commanded us; and we came to Kadesh-barnea.

20. And I said unto you: Ye are come unto the hill-country of the Amorites, which the LORD our God giveth unto us.

21. Behold, the LORD thy God hath set the land before thee; go up, take possession, as the LORD, the God of thy fathers, hath spoken unto thee; fear not, neither be dismayed.

22. And ye came near unto me every one of you, and said: Let us send men before us, that they may search the land for us, and bring us back word of the way by which we must go up, and the cities unto which we shall come.

23. And the thing pleased me well; and I took twelve men of you, one man for every tribe;

24. And they turned and went up into the mountains, and came unto the valley of Eshcol, and spied it out.

25. And they took of the fruit of the land in their hands, and brought it down unto us, and brought us back word, and said: Good is the land which the LORD our God giveth unto us.

26. Yet ye would not go up, but rebelled against the commandment of the LORD your God;

27. And ye murmured in your tents, and said: Because the LORD hated us, He hath brought us forth out of the land of Egypt, to deliver us into the hand of the Amorites, to destroy us.

28. Whither are we going up? our brethren have made our heart to melt, saying: The people is greater and taller than we; the cities are great and fortified up to heaven; and moreover we have seen the sons of the Anakim there.

29. Then I said unto you: Dread not, neither be afraid of them.

30. The LORD your God who goeth before you, He shall fight for you, according to all that He did for you in Egypt before your eyes;

31. And in the wilderness, where thou hast seen how that the LORD thy God bore thee, as a man doth bear his son, in all the way that ye went, until ye came unto this place.

32. Yet in this thing ye do not believe the LORD your God,

33. Who went before you in the way, to seek you out a place to pitch your tents in: in fire by night, to show you by what way ye should go, and in the cloud by day.

34. And the LORD heard the voice of your words, and was wroth, and swore, saying:

35. Surely there shall not one of these men, even this evil generation, see the good land, which I swore to give unto your fathers,

36. Save Caleb the son of Jephunneh, he shall see it; and to him will I give the land that he hath trodden upon, and to his children; because he hath wholly followed the LORD.

37. Also, the LORD was angry with me for your sakes, saying: Thou also shalt not go in thither;

38. Joshua the son of Nun, who standeth before thee, he shall go in thither; encourage thou him, for he shall cause Israel to inherit it.

39. Moreover, your little ones, that ye said should be a prey, and your children, that this day have no knowledge of good or evil, they shall go in thither, and unto them will I give it, and they shall possess it.

40. But as for you, turn you, and take your journey into the wilderness by the way to the Red Sea.

41. Then ye answered and said unto me: We have sinned against the LORD, we will go up and fight, according to all that the LORD our God commanded us. And ye girded on every man his weapons of war, and deemed it a light thing to go up into the hill-country.

42. And the LORD said unto me: Say unto them: Go not up, neither fight; for I am not among you; lest ye be smitten before your enemies.

43. So, I spoke unto you, and ye hearkened not; but ye rebelled against the commandment of the LORD, and were presumptuous, and went up into the hill-country.

44. And the Amorites, that dwell in that hill-country, came out against you, and chased you, as bees do, and beat you down in Seir, even unto Hormah.

45. And ye returned and wept before the LORD; but the LORD hearkened not to your voice, nor gave ear unto you.

46. So ye abode in Kadesh many days, according unto the days that ye abode there.

Chapter 2

1. Then we turned, and took our journey into the wilderness by the way to the Red Sea, as the LORD spoke unto me; and we compassed mount Seir many days.

2. And the LORD spoke unto me, saying:

3. Ye have compassed this mountain long enough; turn you northward.

4. And command thou the people, saying: Ye are to pass through the border of your brethren the children of Esau, that dwell in Seir; and they will be afraid of you; take ye good heed unto yourselves therefore;

5. Contend not with them; for I will not give you of their land, no, not so much as for the sole of the foot to tread on; because I have given mount Seir unto

Esau for a possession.

6. Ye shall purchase food of them for money, that ye may eat; and ye shall also buy water of them for money, that ye may drink.

7. For the LORD thy God hath blessed thee in all the work of thy hand; He hath known thy walking through this great wilderness; these forty years the LORD thy God hath been with thee; thou hast lacked nothing.

8. So, we passed by from our brethren the children of Esau, that dwell in Seir, from the way of the Arabah, from Elath and from Ezion-geber. And we turned and passed by the way of the wilderness of Moab.

9. And the LORD said unto me: Be not at enmity with Moab, neither contend with them in battle; for I will not give thee of his land for a possession; because I have given Ar unto the children of Lot for a possession.

10. The Emim dwelt therein aforetime, a people great, and many, and tall, as the Anakim;

11. These also are accounted Rephaim, as the Anakim; but the Moabites call them Emim.

12. And in Seir dwelt the Horites aforetime, but the children of Esau succeeded them; and they destroyed them from before them, and dwelt in their stead; as Israel did unto the land of his possession, which the LORD gave unto them.

13. Now rise up, and get you over the brook Zered. And we went over the brook Zered.

14. And the days in which we came from Kadesh-barnea, until we were come over the brook Zered, were thirty and eight years; until all the generation, even the men of war, were consumed from the midst of the camp, as the LORD swore unto them.

15. Moreover, the hand of the LORD was against them, to discomfit them from the midst of the camp, until they were consumed.

16. So it came to pass, when all the men of war were consumed and dead from among the people,

17. That the LORD spoke unto me saying:

18. Thou art this day to pass over the border of Moab, even Ar;

19. And when thou comest nigh over against the children of Ammon, harass them not, nor contend with them; for I will not give thee of the land of the children of Ammon for a possession; because I have given it unto the children of Lot for a possession.

20. That also is accounted a land of Rephaim: Rephaim dwelt therein aforetime; but the Ammonites call them Zamzummim,

21. A people great, and many, and tall, as the Anakim; but the LORD destroyed them before them; and they succeeded them, and dwelt in their stead;

22. As He did for the children of Esau, that dwell in Seir, when He destroyed the Horites from before them; and they succeeded them, and dwelt in their stead even unto this day;

23. And the Avvim, that dwelt in villages as far as

Gaza, the Caphtorim, that came forth out of Caphtor, destroyed them, and dwelt in their stead.

24. Rise ye up, take your journey, and pass over the valley of Arnon; behold, I have given into thy hand Sihon the Amorite, king of Heshbon, and his land; begin to possess it, and contend with him in battle.

25. This day will I begin to put the dread of thee and the fear of thee upon the peoples that are under the whole heaven, who, when they hear the report of thee, shall tremble, and be in anguish because of thee.

26. And I sent messengers out of the wilderness of Kedemoth unto Sihon king of Heshbon with words of peace, saying:

27. Let me pass through thy land; I will go along by the highway, I will neither turn unto the right hand nor to the left.

28. Thou shalt sell me food for money, that I may eat; and give me water for money, that I may drink; only let me pass through on my feet;

29. As the children of Esau that dwell in Seir, and the Moabites that dwell in Ar, did unto me; until I shall pass over the Jordan into the land which the LORD our God giveth us.

30. But Sihon king of Heshbon would not let us pass by him; for the LORD thy God hardened his spirit, and made his heart obstinate, that He might deliver him into thy hand, as appeareth this day.

31. And the LORD said unto me: Behold, I have begun to deliver up Sihon and his land before thee;

begin to possess his land.

32. Then Sihon came out against us, he and all his people, unto battle at Jahaz.

33. And the LORD our God delivered him up before us; and we smote him, and his sons, and all his people.

34. And we took all his cities at that time, and utterly destroyed every city, the men, and the women, and the little ones; we left none remaining;

35. Only the cattle we took for a prey unto ourselves, with the spoil of the cities which we had taken.

36. From Aroer, which is on the edge of the valley of Arnon, and from the city that is in the valley, even unto Gilead, there was not a city too high for us: the LORD our God delivered up all before us.

37. Only to the land of the children of Ammon thou Camest not near; all the side of the river Jabbok, and the cities of the hill-country, and wheresoever the LORD our God forbade us.

Chapter 3

1. Then we turned, and went up the way to Bashan; and Og the king of Bashan came out against us, he and all his people, unto battle at Edrei.

2. And the LORD said unto me: Fear him not; for I have delivered him, and all his people, and his land, into thy hand; and thou shalt do unto him as thou didst unto Sihon king of the Amorites, who dwelt at Heshbon.

3. So, the LORD our God delivered into our hand Og

also, the king of Bashan, and all his people; and we smote him until none was left to him remaining.

4. And we took all his cities at that time; there was not a city which we took not from them; threescore cities, all the region of Argob, the kingdom of Og in Bashan.

5. All these were fortified cities, with high walls, gates, and bars; beside the unwalled towns a great many.

6. And we utterly destroyed them, as we did unto Sihon king of Heshbon, utterly destroying every city, the men, and the women, and the little ones.

7. But all the cattle, and the spoil of the cities, we took for a prey unto ourselves.

8. And we took the land at that time out of the hand of the two kings of the Amorites that were beyond the Jordan, from the valley of Arnon unto mount Hermon.

9. Which Hermon the Sidonians call Sirion, and the Amorites call it Senir.

10. All the cities of the plain, and all Gilead, and all Bashan, unto Salcah and Edrei, cities of the kingdom of Og in Bashan.

11. For only Og king of Bashan remained of the remnant of the Rephaim; behold, his bedstead was a bedstead of iron; is it not in Rabbah of the children of Ammon? nine cubits was the length thereof, and four cubits the breadth of it, after the cubit of a man.

12. And this land we took in possession at that time;

from Aroer, which is by the valley of Arnon, and half the hill-country of Gilead, and the cities thereof, gave I unto the Reubenites and to the Gadites;

13. And the rest of Gilead, and all Bashan, the kingdom of Og, gave I unto the half-tribe of Manasseh; all the region of Argob-all that Bashan is called the land of Rephaim.

14. Jair the son of Manasseh took all the region of Argob, unto the border of the Geshurites and the Maacathites, and called them, even Bashan, after his own name, Havvoth-jair, unto this day.

15. And I gave Gilead unto Machir.

16. And unto the Reubenites and unto the Gadites I gave from Gilead even unto the valley of Arnon, the middle of the valley for a border; even unto the river Jabbok, which is the border of the children of Ammon;

17. The Arabah also, the Jordan being the border thereof, from Chinnereth even unto the sea of the Arabah, the Salt Sea, under the slopes of Pisgah eastward.

18. And I commanded you at that time, saying: The LORD your God hath given you this land to possess it; ye shall pass over armed before your brethren the children of Israel, all the men of valour.

19. But your wives, and your little ones, and your cattle-I know that ye have much cattle-shall abide in your cities which I have given you;

20. Until the LORD give rest unto your brethren, as

unto you, and they also possess the land which the LORD your God giveth them beyond the Jordan; then shall ye return every man unto his possession, which I have given you.

21. And I commanded Joshua at that time, saying: Thine eyes have seen all that the LORD your God hath done unto these two kings; so, shall the LORD do unto all the kingdoms whither thou goest over.

22. Ye shall not fear them; for the LORD your God, He it is that fighteth for you.

Vaetchanan

23. And I besought the LORD at that time, saying:

24. O Lord GOD, thou hast begun to show Thy servant Thy greatness, and thy strong hand; for what god is there in heaven or on earth, that can do according to Thy works, and according to Thy mighty acts?

25. Let me go over, I pray Thee, and see the good land that is beyond the Jordan, that goodly hill-country, and Lebanon.

26. But the LORD was wroth with me for your sakes, and hearkened not unto me; and the LORD said unto me: Let it suffice thee; speak no more unto Me of this matter.

27. Get thee up into the top of Pisgah, and lift up thine eyes westward, and northward, and southward, and eastward, and behold with thine eyes; for thou shalt not go over this Jordan.

28. But charge Joshua, and encourage him, and strengthen him; for he shall go over before this people, and he shall cause them to inherit the land which thou shalt see.

29. So, we abode in the valley over against Beth-peor.

Chapter 4

1. And now, O Israel, hearken unto the statutes and unto the ordinances, which I teach you, to do them; that ye may live, and go in and possess the land which the LORD, the God of your fathers, giveth you.

2. Ye shall not add unto the word which I command you, neither shall ye diminish from it, that ye may keep the commandments of the LORD your God which I command you.

3. Your eyes have seen what the LORD did in Baal-peor; for all the men that followed the Baal of Peor, the LORD thy God hath destroyed them from the midst of thee.

4. But ye that did cleave unto the LORD your God are alive every one of you this day.

5. Behold, I have taught you statutes and ordinances, even as the LORD my God commanded me, that ye should do so in the midst of the land whither ye go in to possess it.

6. Observe therefore and do them; for this is your wisdom and your understanding in the sight of the peoples, that, when they hear all these statutes, shall say: Surely this great nation is a wise and understanding people.

7. For what great nation is there, that hath God so nigh unto them, as the LORD our God is whensoever we call upon Him?

8. And what great nation is there, that hath statutes and ordinances so righteous as all this law, which I set before you this day?

9. Only take heed to thyself, and keep thy soul diligently, lest thou forget the things which thine eyes saw, and lest they depart from thy heart all the days of thy life; but make them known unto thy children and thy children's children;

10. The day that thou stoodest before the LORD thy God in Horeb, when the LORD said unto me: Assemble Me the people, and I will make them hear My words that they may learn to fear Me all the days that they live upon the earth, and that they may teach their children.

11. And ye came near and stood under the mountain; and the mountain burned with fire unto the heart of heaven, with darkness, cloud, and thick darkness.

12. And the LORD spoke unto you out of the midst of the fire; ye heard the voice of words, but ye saw no form; only a voice.

13. And He declared unto you His covenant, which He commanded you to perform, even the ten words; and He wrote them upon two tables of stone.

14. And the LORD commanded me at that time to

teach you statutes and ordinances, that ye might do them in the land whither ye go over to possess it.

15. Take ye therefore good heed unto yourselves-for ye saw no manner of form on the day that the LORD spoke unto you in Horeb out of the midst of the fire.

16. Lest ye deal corruptly, and make you a graven image, even the form of any figure, the likeness of male or female,

17. The likeness of any beast that is on the earth, the likeness of any winged fowl that flieth in the heaven,

18. The likeness of any thing that creepeth on the ground, the likeness of any fish that is in the water under the earth;

19. And lest thou lift up thine eyes unto heaven, and when thou seest the sun and the moon and the stars, even all the host of heaven, thou be drawn away and worship them, and serve them, which the LORD thy God hath allotted unto all the peoples under the whole heaven.

20. But you hath the LORD taken and brought forth out of the iron furnace, out of Egypt, to be unto Him a people of inheritance, as ye are this day.

21. Now the LORD was angered with me for your sakes, and swore that I should not go over the Jordan, and that I should not go in unto that good land, which the LORD thy God giveth thee for an inheritance;

22. But I must die in this land, I must not go over the Jordan; but ye are to go over, and possess that good land.

23. Take heed unto yourselves, lest ye forget the covenant of the LORD your God, which He made with you, and make you a graven image, even the likeness of any thing which the LORD thy God hath forbidden thee.

24. For the LORD thy God is a devouring fire, a jealous God.

25. When thou shalt beget children, and children's children, and ye shall have been long in the land, and shall deal corruptly, and make a graven image, even the form of any thing, and shall do that which is evil in the sight of the LORD thy God, to provoke Him;

26. I call heaven and earth to witness against you this day, that ye shall soon utterly perish from off the land whereunto ye go over the Jordan to possess it; ye shall not prolong your days upon it, but shall utterly be destroyed.

27. And the LORD shall scatter you among the peoples, and ye shall be left few in number among the nations, whither the LORD shall lead you away.

28. And there ye shall serve gods, the work of men's hands, wood and stone, which neither see, nor hear, nor eat, nor smell.

29. But from thence ye will seek the LORD thy God; and thou shalt find Him, if thou search after Him with all thy heart and with all thy soul.

30. In thy distress, when all these things are come upon thee, in the end of days, thou wilt return to the LORD thy God, and hearken unto His voice;

31. For the LORD thy God is a merciful God; He will not fail thee, neither destroy thee, nor forget the covenant of thy fathers which He swore unto them.

32. For ask now of the days past, which were before thee, since the day that God created man upon the earth, and from the one end of heaven unto the other, whether there hath been any such thing as this great thing is, or hath been heard like it?

33. Did ever a people hear the voice of God speaking out of the midst of the fire, as thou hast heard, and live?

34. Or hath God assayed to go and take Him a nation from the midst of another nation, by trials, by signs, and by wonders, and by war, and by a mighty hand, and by an outstretched arm, and by great terrors, according to all that the LORD your God did for you in Egypt before thine eyes?

35. Unto thee it was shown, that thou mightiest know that the LORD, He is God; there is none else beside Him.

36. Out of heaven He made thee to hear His voice, that He might instruct thee; and upon earth He made thee to see His great fire; and thou didst hear His words out of the midst of the fire.

37. And because He loved thy fathers, and chose their seed after them, and brought thee out with His presence, with His great power, out of Egypt,

38. To drive out nations from before thee greater and mightier than thou, to bring thee in, to give thee their land for an inheritance, as it is this day;

39. Know this day, and lay it to thy heart, that the LORD, He is God in heaven above and upon the earth beneath; there is none else.

40. And thou shalt keep His statutes, and His commandments, which I command thee this day, that it may go well with thee, and with thy children after thee, and that thou mayest prolong thy days upon the land, which the LORD thy God giveth thee, for ever.

41. Then Moses separated three cities beyond the Jordan toward the sunrising;

42. That the manslayer might flee thither, that slayeth his neighbour unawares, and hated him not in time past; and that fleeing unto one of these cities he might live:

43. Bezer in the wilderness, in the table-land, for the Reubenites; and Ramoth in Gilead, for the Gadites; and Golan in Bashan, for the Manassites.

44. And this is the law which Moses set before the children of Israel;

45. These are the testimonies, and the statutes, and the ordinances, which Moses spoke unto the children of Israel, when they came forth out of Egypt;

46. Beyond the Jordan, in the valley over against Beth-peor, in the land of Sihon king of the Amorites, who dwelt at Heshbon, whom Moses and the children of Israel smote, when they came forth out of Egypt;

47. And they took his land in possession, and the land of Og king of Bashan, the two kings of the Amorites, who were beyond the Jordan toward the sunrising;

48. From Aroer, which is on the edge of the valley of Arnon, even unto mount Sion-the same is Hermon.

49. And all the Arabah beyond the Jordan eastward, even unto the sea of the Arabah, under the slopes of Pisgah.

Chapter 5

1. And Moses called unto all Israel, and said unto them: Hear, O Israel, the statutes and the ordinances which I speak in your ears this day, that ye may learn them, and observe to do them.

2. The LORD our God made a covenant with us in Horeb.

3. The LORD made not this covenant with our fathers, but with us, even us, who are all of us here alive this day.

4. The LORD spoke with you face to face in the mount out of the midst of the fire.

5. I stood between the LORD and you at that time, to declare unto you the word of the LORD; for ye were afraid because of the fire, and went not up into the mount-saying:

6. I am the LORD thy God, who brought thee out of the land of Egypt, out of the house of bondage.

7. Thou shalt have no other gods before Me.

8. Thou shalt not make unto thee a graven image, even any manner of likeness, of any thing that is in heaven above, or that is in the earth beneath, or that is in the water under the earth.

9. Thou shalt not bow down unto them, nor serve them; for I the LORD thy God am a jealous God, visiting the iniquity of the fathers upon the children, and upon the third and upon the fourth generation of them that hate Me,

10. And showing mercy unto the thousandth generation of them that love Me and keep My commandments.

11. Thou shalt not take the name of the LORD thy God in vain; for the LORD will not hold him guiltless that taketh His name in vain.

12. Observe the sabbath day, to keep it holy, as the LORD thy God commanded thee.

13. Six days shalt thou labour, and do all thy work;

14. But the seventh day is a sabbath unto the LORD thy God, in it thou shalt not do any manner of work, thou, nor thy son, nor thy daughter, nor thy man-servant, nor thy maid-servant, nor thine ox, nor thine ass, nor any of thy cattle, nor thy stranger that is within thy gates; that thy man-servant and thy maid-servant may rest as well as thou.

15. And thou shalt remember that thou was a servant in the land of Egypt, and the LORD thy God brought thee out thence by a mighty hand and by an outstretched arm; therefore the LORD thy God commanded thee to keep the sabbath day.

16. Honour thy father and thy mother, as the LORD thy God commanded thee; that thy days may be long, and that it may go well with thee, upon the land which the LORD thy God giveth thee.

17. Thou shalt not murder. Neither shalt thou commit adultery. Neither shalt thou steal. Neither shalt thou bear false witness against thy neighbour.

18. Neither shalt thou covet thy neighbour's wife; neither shalt thou desire thy neighbour's house, his field, or his man-servant, or his maid-servant, his ox, or his ass, or any thing that is thy neighbour's.

19. These words the LORD spoke unto all your assembly in the mount out of the midst of the fire, of the cloud, and of the thick darkness, with a great voice, and it went on no more. And He wrote them upon two tables of stone, and gave them unto me.

20. And it came to pass, when ye heard the voice out of the midst of the darkness, while the mountain did burn with fire, that ye came near unto me, even all the heads of your tribes, and your elders;

21. And ye said: Behold, the LORD our God hath shown us His glory and His greatness, and we have heard His voice out of the midst of the fire; we have seen this day that God doth speak with man, and he liveth.

22. Now therefore why should we die? for this great fire will consume us; if we hear the voice of the LORD our God any more, then we shall die.

23. For who is there of all flesh, that hath heard the voice of the living God speaking out of the midst of the fire, as we have, and lived?

24. Go thou near, and hear all that the LORD our God may say; and thou shalt speak unto us all that the LORD our God may speak unto thee; and we will hear it and do it.

25. And the LORD heard the voice of your words, when ye spoke unto me; and the LORD said unto me: I have heard the voice of the words of this people, which they have spoken unto thee; they have well said all that they have spoken.

26. Oh, that they had such a heart as this alway, to fear Me, and keep all My commandments, that it might be well with them, and with their children for ever!

27. Go say to them: Return ye to your tents.

28. But as for thee, stand thou here by Me, and I will speak unto thee all the commandment, and the statutes, and the ordinances, which thou shalt teach them, that they may do them in the land which I give them to possess it.

29. Ye shall observe to do therefore as the LORD your God hath commanded you; ye shall not turn aside to the right hand or to the left.

30. Ye shall walk in all the way which the LORD your God hath commanded you, that ye may live, and that it may be well with you, and that ye may prolong your days in the land which ye shall possess.

Chapter 6

1. Now this is the commandment, the statutes, and the

ordinances, which the LORD your God commanded to teach you, that ye might do them in the land whither ye go over to possess it.

2. That thou mightest fear the LORD thy God, to keep all His statutes and His commandments, which I command thee, thou, and thy son, and thy son's son, all the days of thy life; and that thy days may be prolonged.

3. Hear therefore, O Israel, and observe to do it; that it may be well with thee, and that ye may increase mightily, as the LORD, the God of thy fathers, hath promised unto thee-a land flowing with milk and honey.

4. HEAR, O ISRAEL: THE LORD OUR GOD, THE LORD IS ONE.

5. And thou shalt love the LORD thy God with all thy heart, and with all thy soul, and with all thy might.

6. And these words, which I command thee this day, shall be upon thy heart;

7. And thou shalt teach them diligently unto thy children, and shalt talk of them when thou sittest in thy house, and when thou walkest by the way, and when thou liest down, and when thou risest up.

8. And thou shalt bind them for a sign upon thy hand, and they shall be for frontlets between thine eyes.

9. And thou shalt write them upon the door-posts of thy house, and upon thy gates.

10. And it shall be, when the LORD thy God shall bring thee into the land which He swore unto thy fathers, to Abraham, to Isaac, and to Jacob, to give thee-great and goodly cities, which thou didst not build,

11. And houses full of all good things, which thou didst not fill, and cisterns hewn out, which thou the didst not hew, vineyards and olive-trees, which thou didst not plant, and thou shalt eat and be satisfied.

12. Then beware lest thou forget the LORD, who brought thee forth out of the land of Egypt, out of the house of bondage.

13. Thou shalt fear the LORD thy God; and Him shalt thou serve, and by His name shalt thou swear.

14. Ye shall not go after other gods, of the gods of the peoples that are round about you;

15. For a jealous God, even the LORD thy God, is in the midst of thee; lest the anger of the LORD thy God be kindled against thee, and He destroy thee from off the face of the earth.

16. Ye shall not try the LORD your God, as ye tried Him in Massah.

17. Ye shall diligently keep the commandments of the LORD your God, and His testimonies, and His statutes, which He hath commanded thee.

18. And thou shalt do that which is right and good in the sight of the LORD; that it may be well with thee, and that thou mayest go in and possess the good land which the LORD swore unto thy fathers,

19. To thrust out all thine enemies from before thee, as the LORD hath spoken.

20. When thy son asketh thee in time to come, saying: What mean the testimonies, and the statutes, and the ordinances, which the LORD our God hath commanded you?

21. Then thou shalt say unto thy son: We were Pharaoh's bondmen in Egypt; and the LORD brought us out of Egypt with a mighty hand.

22. And the LORD showed signs and wonders, great and sore, upon Egypt, upon Pharaoh, and upon all his house, before our eyes.

23. And He brought us out from thence, that He might bring us in, to give us the land which He swore unto our fathers.

24. And the LORD commanded us to do all these statutes, to fear the LORD our God, for our good always, that He might preserve us alive, as it is at this day.

25. And it shall be righteousness unto us, if we observe to do all this commandment before the LORD our God, as He hath commanded us.

Chapter 7

1. When the LORD thy God shall bring thee into the land whither, thou goest to possess it, and shall cast out many nations before thee, the Hittite, and the Girgashite, and the Amorite, and the Canaanite, and the Perizzite, and the Hivite, and the Jebusite, seven nations greater and mightier than thou;

2. And when the LORD thy God shall deliver them

up before thee, and thou shalt smite them; then thou shalt utterly destroy them; thou shalt make no covenant with them, nor show mercy unto them;

3. Neither shalt thou make marriages with them: thy daughter thou shalt not give unto his son, nor his daughter shalt thou take unto thy son.

4. For he will turn away thy son from following Me, that they may serve other gods; so, will the anger of the LORD be kindled against you, and He will destroy thee quickly.

5. But thus, shall ye deal with them: ye shall break down their altars, and dash in pieces their pillars, and hew down their Asherim, and burn their graven images with fire.

6. For thou art a holy people unto the LORD thy God: the LORD thy God hath chosen thee to be His own treasure, out of all peoples that are upon the face of the earth.

7. The LORD did not set His love upon you, nor choose you, because ye were more in number than any people-for ye were the fewest of all peoples.

8. But because the LORD loved you, and because He would keep the oath which He swore unto your fathers, hath the LORD brought you out with a mighty hand, and redeemed you out of the house of bondage, from the hand of Pharaoh king of Egypt.

9. Know therefore that the LORD thy God, He is God; the faithful God, who keepeth covenant and mercy with them that love Him and keep His commandments to a thousand generations;

10. And repayeth them that hate Him to their face, to destroy them; He will not be slack to him that hateth Him, He will repay him to his face.

11. Thou shalt therefore keep the commandment, and the statutes, and the ordinances, which I command thee this day, to do them.

Eikev

12. And it shall come to pass, because ye hearken to these ordinances, and keep, and do them, that the LORD thy God shall keep with thee the covenant and the mercy which He swore unto thy fathers,

13. And He will love thee, and bless thee, and multiply thee; He will also bless the fruit of thy body and the fruit of thy land, thy corn and thy wine and thine oil, the increase of thy kine and the young of thy flock, in the land which He swore unto thy fathers to give thee.

14. Thou shalt be blessed above all peoples; there shall not be male or female barren among you, or among your cattle.

15. And the LORD will take away from thee all sickness; and He will put none of the evil diseases of Egypt, which thou knowest, upon thee, but will lay them upon all them that hate thee.

16. And thou shalt consume all the peoples that the LORD thy God shall deliver unto thee; thine eye shall not pity them; neither shalt thou serve their gods; for that will be a snare unto thee.

17. If thou shalt say in thy heart: These nations are more than I; how can I dispossess them?

18. Thou shalt not be afraid of them; thou shalt well remember what the LORD thy God did unto Pharaoh, and unto all Egypt:

19. The great trials which thine eyes saw, and the signs, and the wonders, and the mighty hand, and the outstretched arm, whereby the LORD thy God brought thee out; so, shall the LORD thy God do unto all the peoples of whom thou art afraid.

20. Moreover, the LORD thy God will send the hornet among them, until they that are left, and they that hide themselves, perish from before thee.

21. Thou shalt not be affrighted at them; for the LORD thy God is in the midst of thee, a God great and awful.

22. And the LORD thy God will cast out those nations before thee by little and little; thou mayest not consume them quickly, lest the beasts of the field increase upon thee.

23. But the LORD thy God shall deliver them up before thee, and shall discomfit them with a great discomfiture, until they be destroyed.

24. And He shall deliver their kings into thy hand, and thou shalt make their name to perish from under heaven; there shall no man be able to stand against thee, until thou have destroyed them.

25. The graven images of their gods shall ye burn with fire; thou shalt not covet the silver or the gold that is on them, nor take it unto thee, lest thou be snared therein; for it is an abomination to the LORD thy God.

26. And thou shalt not bring an abomination into thy house, and be accursed like unto it; thou shalt utterly detest it, and thou shalt utterly abhor it; for it is a devoted thing.

Chapter 8

1. All the commandment which I command thee this day shall ye observe to do, that ye may live, and multiply, and go in and possess the land which the LORD swore unto your fathers.

2. And thou shalt remember all the way which the LORD thy God hath led thee these forty years in the wilderness, that He might afflict thee, to prove thee, to know what was in thy heart, whether thou wouldest keep His commandments, or no.

3. And He afflicted thee, and suffered thee to hunger, and fed thee with manna, which thou knewest not, neither did thy fathers know; that He might make thee know that man doth not live by bread only, but by every thing that proceedeth out of the mouth of the LORD doth man live.

4. Thy raiment waxed not old upon thee, neither did thy foot swell, these forty years.

5. And thou shalt consider in thy heart, that, as a man

chasteneth his son, so the LORD thy God chasteneth thee.

6. And thou shalt keep the commandments of the LORD thy God, to walk in His ways, and to fear Him.

7. For the LORD thy God bringeth thee into a good land, a land of brooks of water, of fountains and depths, springing forth in valleys and hills;

8. A land of wheat and barley, and vines and fig-trees and pomegranates; a land of olive-trees and honey;

9. A land wherein thou shalt eat bread without scarceness, thou shalt not lack any thing in it; a land whose stones are iron, and out of whose hills thou mayest dig brass.

10. And thou shalt eat and be satisfied, and bless the LORD thy God for the good land which He hath given thee.

11. Beware lest thou forget the LORD thy God, in not keeping His commandments, and His ordinances, and His statutes, which I command thee this day;

12. lest when thou hast eaten and art satisfied, and hast built goodly houses, and dwelt therein;

13. And when thy herds and thy flocks multiply, and thy silver and thy gold is multiplied, and all that thou hast is multiplied;

14. Then thy heart be lifted up, and thou forget the LORD thy God, who brought thee forth out of the land of Egypt, out of the house of bondage;

15. Who led thee through the great and dreadful wilderness, wherein were serpents, fiery serpents, and scorpions, and thirsty ground where was no water; who brought thee forth water out of the rock of flint;

16. Who fed thee in the wilderness with manna, which thy fathers knew not, that He might afflict thee, and that He might prove thee, to do thee good at thy latter end;

17. And thou say in thy heart: My power and the might of my hand hath gotten me this wealth.

18. But thou shalt remember the LORD thy God, for it is He that giveth thee power to get wealth, that He may establish His covenant which He swore unto thy fathers, as it is this day.

19. And it shall be, if thou shalt forget the LORD thy God, and walk after other gods, and serve them, and worship them, I forewarn you this day that ye shall surely perish.

20. As the nations that the LORD maketh to perish before you, so shall ye perish; because ye would not hearken unto the voice of the LORD your God.

Chapter 9

1. Hear, O Israel: thou art to pass over the Jordan this day, to go in to dispossess nations greater and mightier than thyself, cities great and fortified up to heaven,

2. A people great and tall, the sons of the Anakim, whom thou knowest, and of whom thou hast heard say: Who can stand before the sons of Anak?

3. Know therefore this day, that the LORD thy God

is He who goeth over before thee as a devouring fire; He will destroy them, and He will bring them down before thee; so shalt thou drive them out, and make them to perish quickly, as the LORD hath spoken unto thee.

4. Speak not thou in thy heart, after that the LORD thy God hath thrust them out from before thee, saying: For my righteousness the LORD hath brought me in to possess this land; whereas for the wickedness of these nations the LORD doth drive them out from before thee.

5. Not for thy righteousness, or for the uprightness of thy heart, dost thou go in to possess their land; but for the wickedness of these nations the LORD thy God doth drive them out from before thee, and that He may establish the word which the LORD swore unto thy fathers, to Abraham, to Isaac, and to Jacob.

6. Know therefore that it is not for thy righteousness that the LORD thy God giveth thee this good land to possess it; for thou art a stiffnecked people.

7. Remember, forget thou not, how thou didst make the LORD thy God wroth in the wilderness; from the day that thou didst go forth out of the land of Egypt, until ye came unto this place, ye have been rebellious against the LORD.

8. Also, in Horeb ye made the LORD wroth, and the LORD was angered with you to have destroyed you.

9. When I was gone up into the mount to receive the tables of stone, even the tables of the covenant which the LORD made with you, then I abode in the mount forty days and forty nights; I did neither eat bread nor drink water.

10. And the LORD delivered unto me the two tables of stone written with the finger of God; and on them was written according to all the words, which the LORD spoke with you in the mount out of the midst of the fire in the day of the assembly.

11. And it came to pass at the end of forty days and forty nights, that the LORD gave me the two tables of stone, even the tables of the covenant.

12. And the LORD said unto me: Arise, get thee down quickly from hence; for thy people that thou hast brought forth out of Egypt have dealt corruptly; they are quickly turned aside out of the way which I commanded them; they have made them a molten image.

13. Furthermore, the LORD spoke unto me, saying: I have seen this people, and, behold, it is a stiffnecked people;

14. Let Me alone, that I may destroy them, and blot out their name from under heaven; and I will make of thee a nation mightier and greater than they.

15. So, I turned and came down from the mount, and the mount burned with fire; and the two tables of the covenant were in my two hands.

16. And I looked, and, behold, ye had sinned against the LORD your God; ye had made you a molten calf; ye had turned aside quickly out of the way which the

LORD had commanded you.

17. And I took hold of the two tables, and cast them out of my two hands, and broke them before your eyes.

18. And I fell down before the LORD, as at the first, forty days and forty nights; I did neither eat bread nor drink water; because of all your sin which ye sinned, in doing that which was evil in the sight of the LORD, to provoke Him.

19. For I was in dread of the anger and hot displeasure, wherewith the LORD was wroth against you to destroy you. But the LORD hearkened unto me that time also.

20. Moreover, the LORD was very angry with Aaron to have destroyed him; and I prayed for Aaron also the same time.

21. And I took your sin, the calf which ye had made, and burnt it with fire, and beat it in pieces, grinding it very small, until it was as fine as dust; and I cast the dust thereof into the brook that descended out of the mount.

22. And at Taberah, and at Massah, and at Kibroth-hattaavah, ye made the LORD wroth.

23. And when the LORD sent you from Kadesh-barnea, saying: Go up and possess the land which I have given you; then ye rebelled against the commandment of the LORD your God, and ye believed Him not, nor hearkened to His voice.

24. Ye have been rebellious against the LORD from

the day that I knew you.

25. So, I fell down before the LORD the forty days and forty nights that I fell down; because the LORD had said He would destroy you.

26. And I prayed unto the LORD, and said: O Lord GOD, destroy not Thy people and Thine inheritance, that Thou hast redeemed through Thy greatness, that Thou hast brought forth out of Egypt with a mighty hand.

27. Remember Thy servants, Abraham, Isaac, and Jacob; look not unto the stubbornness of this people, nor to their wickedness, nor to their sin;

28. Lest the land whence Thou broughtest us out say: Because the LORD was not able to bring them into the land which He promised unto them, and because He hated them, He hath brought them out to slay them in the wilderness.

29. Yet they are Thy people and Thine inheritance, that Thou didst bring out by Thy great power and by Thy outstretched arm.

Chapter 10

1. At that time the LORD said unto me: Hew thee two tables of stone like unto the first, and come up unto Me into the mount; and make thee an ark of wood.

2. And I will write on the tables the words that were on the first tables which thou didst break, and thou shalt put them in the ark.

3. So, I made an ark of acacia-wood, and hewed two

tables of stone like unto the first, and went up into the mount, having the two tables in my hand.

4. And He wrote on the tables according to the first writing, the ten words, which the LORD spoke unto you in the mount out of the midst of the fire in the day of the assembly; and the LORD gave them unto me.

5. And I turned and came down from the mount, and put the tables in the ark which I had made; and there they are, as the LORD commanded me.

6. And the children of Israel journeyed from Beeroth-benejaakan to Moserah; there Aaron died, and there he was buried; and Eleazar his son ministered in the priest's office in his stead.

7. From thence they journeyed unto Gudgod; and from Gudgod to Jotbah, a land of brooks of water.

8. At that time the LORD separated the tribe of Levi, to bear the ark of the covenant of the LORD, to stand before the LORD to minister unto Him, and to bless in His name, unto this day.

9. Wherefore Levi hath no portion nor inheritance with his brethren; the LORD is his inheritance, according as the LORD thy God spoke unto him.

10. Now I stayed in the mount, as at the first time, forty days and forty nights; and the LORD hearkened unto me that time also; the LORD would not destroy thee.

11. And the LORD said unto me: Arise, go before the people, causing them to set forward, that they may go in and possess the land, which I swore unto their fathers to give unto them.

12. And now, Israel, what doth the LORD thy God require of thee, but to fear the LORD thy God, to walk in all His ways, and to love Him, and to serve the LORD thy God with all thy heart and with all thy soul;

13. To keep for thy good the commandments of the LORD, and His statutes, which I command thee this day?

14. Behold, unto the LORD thy God belongeth the heaven, and the heaven of heavens, the earth, with all that therein is.

15. Only the LORD had a delight in thy fathers to love them, and He chose their seed after them, even you, above all peoples, as it is this day.

16. Circumcise therefore the foreskin of your heart, and be no more stiffnecked.

17. For the LORD your God, He is God of gods, and Lord of lords, the great God, the mighty, and the awful, who regardeth not persons, nor taketh reward.

18. He doth execute justice for the fatherless and widow, and loveth the stranger, in giving him food and raiment.

19. Love ye therefore the stranger; for ye were strangers in the land of Egypt.

20. Thou shalt fear the LORD thy God; Him shalt thou serve; and to Him shalt thou cleave, and by His name shalt thou swear.

21. He is thy glory, and He is thy God, that hath done

for thee these great and tremendous things, which thine eyes have seen.

22. Thy fathers went down into Egypt with threescore and ten persons; and now the LORD thy God hath made thee as the stars of heaven for multitude.

Chapter 11

1. Therefore, thou shalt love the LORD thy God, and keep His charge, and His statutes, and His ordinances, and His commandments, alway.

2. And know ye this day; for I speak not with your children that have not known, and that have not seen the chastisement of the LORD your God, His greatness, His mighty hand, and His outstretched arm,

3. And His signs, and His works, which He did in the midst of Egypt unto Pharaoh the king of Egypt, and unto all his land;

4. And what He did unto the army of Egypt, unto their horses, and to their chariots; how He made the water of the Red Sea to overflow them as they pursued after you, and how the LORD hath destroyed them unto this day;

5. And what He did unto you in the wilderness, until ye came unto this place;

6. And what He did unto Dathan and Abiram, the sons of Eliab, the son of Reuben; how the earth opened her mouth, and swallowed them up, and their households, and their tents, and every living substance that followed them, in the midst of all Israel;

7. But your eyes have seen all the great work of the LORD which He did.

8. Therefore, shall ye keep all the commandment which I command thee this day, that ye may be strong, and go in and possess the land, whither ye go over to possess it;

9. And that ye may prolong your days upon the land, which the LORD swore unto your fathers to give unto them and to their seed, a land flowing with milk and honey.

10. For the land, whither thou goest in to possess it, is not as the land of Egypt, from whence ye came out, where thou didst sow thy seed, and didst water it with thy foot, as a garden of herbs;

11. But the land, whither ye go over to possess it, is a land of hills and valleys, and drinketh water as the rain of heaven cometh down;

12. A land which the LORD thy God careth for; the eyes of the LORD thy God are always upon it, from the beginning of the year even unto the end of the year.

13. And it shall come to pass, if ye shall hearken diligently unto My commandments which I command you this day, to love the LORD your God, and to serve Him with all your heart and with all your soul,

14. That I will give the rain of your land in its season, the former rain and the latter rain, that thou mayest gather in thy corn, and thy wine, and thine oil.

15. And I will give grass in thy fields for thy cattle, and thou shalt eat and be satisfied.

16. Take heed to yourselves, lest your heart be deceived, and ye turn aside, and serve other gods, and worship them;

17. And the anger of the LORD be kindled against you, and He shut up the heaven, so that there shall be no rain, and the ground shall not yield her fruit; and ye perish quickly from off the good land which the LORD giveth you.

18. Therefore, shall ye lay up these My words in your heart and in your soul; and ye shall bind them for a sign upon your hand, and they shall be for frontlets between your eyes.

19. And ye shall teach them your children, talking of them, when thou sittest in thy house, and when thou walkest by the way, and when thou liest down, and when thou risest up.

20. And thou shalt write them upon the door-posts of thy house, and upon thy gates;

21. That your days may be multiplied, and the days of your children, upon the land which the LORD swore unto your fathers to give them, as the days of the heavens above the earth.

22. For if ye shall diligently keep all this commandment which I command you, to do it, to love the LORD your God, to walk in all His ways, and to cleave unto Him,

23. Then will the LORD drive out all these nations

from before you, and ye shall dispossess nations greater and mightier than yourselves.

24. Every place whereon the sole of your foot shall tread shall be yours: from the wilderness, and Lebanon, from the river, the river Euphrates, even unto the hinder sea shall be your border.

25. There shall no man be able to stand against you: the LORD your God shall lay the fear of you and the dread of you upon all the land that ye shall tread upon, as He hath spoken unto you.

Re'eh

26. Behold, I set before you this day a blessing and a curse:

27. The blessing, if ye shall hearken unto the commandments of the LORD your God, which I command you this day;

28. And the curse, if ye shall not hearken unto the commandments of the LORD your God, but turn aside out of the way which I command you this day, to go after other gods, which ye have not known.

29. And it shall come to pass, when the LORD thy God shall bring thee into the land whither, thou goest to possess it, that thou shalt set the blessing upon mount Gerizim, and the curse upon mount Ebal.

30. Are they not beyond the Jordan, behind the way of the going down of the sun, in the land of the Canaanites that dwell in the Arabah, over against

Gilgal, beside the terebinths of Moreh?

31. For ye are to pass over the Jordan to go in to possess the land which the LORD your God giveth you, and ye shall possess it, and dwell therein.

32. And ye shall observe to do all the statutes and the ordinances which I set before you this day.

Chapter 12

1. These are the statutes and the ordinances, which ye shall observe to do in the land which the LORD, the God of thy fathers, hath given thee to possess it, all the days that ye live upon the earth.

2. Ye shall surely destroy all the places, wherein the nations that ye are to dispossess served their gods, upon the high mountains, and upon the hills, and under every leafy tree.

3. And ye shall break down their altars, and dash in pieces their pillars, and burn their Asherim with fire; and ye shall hew down the graven images of their gods; and ye shall destroy their name out of that place.

4. Ye shall not do so unto the LORD your God.

5. But unto the place which the LORD your God shall choose out of all your tribes to put His name there, even unto His habitation shall ye seek, and thither thou shalt come;

6. And thither ye shall bring your burnt-offerings, and your sacrifices, and your tithes, and the offering of your hand, and your vows, and your freewill-offerings, and the firstlings of your herd and of your flock;

7. And there ye shall eat before the LORD your God, and ye shall rejoice in all that ye put your hand unto, ye and your households, wherein the LORD thy God hath blessed thee.

8. Ye shall not do after all that we do here this day, every man whatsoever is right in his own eyes;

9. For ye are not as yet come to the rest and to the inheritance, which the LORD your God giveth thee.

10. But when ye go over the Jordan, and dwell in the land which the LORD your God causeth you to inherit, and He giveth you rest from all your enemies round about, so that ye dwell in safety;

11. Then it shall come to pass that the place which the LORD your God shall choose to cause His name to dwell there, thither shall ye bring all that I command you: your burnt-offerings, and your sacrifices, your tithes, and the offering of your hand, and all your choice vows which ye vow unto the LORD.

12. And ye shall rejoice before the LORD your God, ye, and your sons, and your daughters, and your men-servants, and your maid-servants, and the Levite that is within your gates, forasmuch as he hath no portion nor inheritance with you.

13. Take heed to thyself that thou offer not thy burnt-offerings in every place that thou seest;

14. But in the place which the LORD shall choose in one of thy tribes, there thou shalt offer thy burnt-offerings, and there thou shalt do all that I command thee.

15. Notwithstanding thou mayest kill and eat flesh within all thy gates, after all the desire of thy soul, according to the blessing of the LORD thy God which He hath given thee; the unclean and the clean may eat thereof, as of the gazelle, and as of the hart.

16. Only ye shall not eat the blood; thou shalt pour it out upon the earth as water.

17. Thou mayest not eat within thy gates the tithe of thy corn, or of thy wine, or of thine oil, or the firstlings of thy herd or of thy flock, nor any of thy vows which thou vowest, nor thy freewill-offerings, nor the offering of thy hand;

18. But thou shalt eat them before the LORD thy God in the place which the LORD thy God shall choose, thou, and thy son, and thy daughter, and thy man-servant, and thy maid-servant, and the Levite that is within thy gates; and thou shalt rejoice before the LORD thy God in all that thou puttest thy hand unto.

19. Take heed to thyself that thou forsake not the Levite as long as thou livest upon thy land.

20. When the LORD thy God shall enlarge thy border, as He hath promised thee, and thou shalt say: I will eat flesh, because thy soul desireth to eat flesh; thou mayest eat flesh, after all the desire of thy soul.

21. If the place which the LORD thy God shall choose to put His name there be too far from thee, then thou shalt kill of thy herd and of thy flock, which the

LORD hath given thee, as I have commanded thee, and thou shalt eat within thy gates, after all the desire of thy soul.

22. Howbeit as the gazelle and as the hart is eaten, so thou shalt eat thereof; the unclean and the clean may eat thereof alike.

23. Only be stedfast in not eating the blood; for the blood is the life; and thou shalt not eat the life with the flesh.

24. Thou shalt not eat it; thou shalt pour it out upon the earth as water.

25. Thou shalt not eat it; that it may go well with thee, and with thy children after thee, when thou shalt do that which is right in the eyes of the LORD.

26. Only thy holy things which thou hast, and thy vows, thou shalt take, and go unto the place which the LORD shall choose;

27. And thou shalt offer thy burnt-offerings, the flesh and the blood, upon the altar of the LORD thy God; and the blood of thy sacrifices shall be poured out against the altar of the LORD thy God, and thou shalt eat the flesh.

28. Observe and hear all these words which I command thee, that it may go well with thee, and with thy children after thee for ever, when thou doest that which is good and right in the eyes of the LORD thy God.

29. When the LORD thy God shall cut off the nations from before thee, whither thou goest in to dispossess them, and thou dispossessest them, and dwellest in their land;

30. Take heed to thyself that thou be not ensnared to follow them, after that they are destroyed from before thee; and that thou inquire not after their gods, saying: How used these nations to serve their gods? even so will I do likewise.

31. Thou shalt not do so unto the LORD thy God; for every abomination to the LORD, which He hateth, have they done unto their gods; for even their sons and their daughters do they burn in the fire to their gods.

Chapter 13

1. All this word which I command you, that shall ye observe to do; thou shalt not add thereto, nor diminish from it.

2. If there arise in the midst of thee a prophet, or a dreamer of dreams-and he give thee a sign or a wonder,

3. And the sign or the wonder come to pass, whereof he spoke unto thee-saying: Let us go after other gods, which thou hast not known, and let us serve them;

4. Thou shalt not hearken unto the words of that prophet, or unto that dreamer of dreams; for the LORD your God putteth you to proof, to know whether ye do love the LORD your God with all your heart and with all your soul.

5. After the LORD your God shall ye walk, and Him

shall ye fear, and His commandments shall ye keep, and unto His voice shall ye hearken, and Him shall ye serve, and unto Him shall ye cleave.

6. And that prophet, or that dreamer of dreams, shall be put to death; because he hath spoken perversion against the LORD your God, who brought you out of the land of Egypt, and redeemed thee out of the house of bondage, to draw thee aside out of the way which the LORD thy God commanded thee to walk in. So shalt thou put away the evil from the midst of thee.

7. If thy brother, the son of thy mother, or thy son, or thy daughter, or the wife of thy bosom, or thy friend, that is as thine own soul, entice thee secretly, saying: 'Let us go and serve other gods,' which thou hast not known, thou, nor thy fathers;

8. Of the gods of the peoples that are round about you, nigh unto thee, or far off from thee, from the one end of the earth even unto the other end of the earth;

9. Thou shalt not consent unto him, nor hearken unto him; neither shall thine eye pity him, neither shalt thou spare, neither shalt thou conceal him;

10. But thou shalt surely kill him; thy hand shall be first upon him to put him to death, and afterwards the hand of all the people.

11. And thou shalt stone him with stones, that he die; because he hath sought to draw thee away from the LORD thy God, who brought thee out of the land of Egypt, out of the house of bondage.

12. And all Israel shall hear, and fear, and shall do no more any such wickedness as this is in the midst of thee.

13. If thou shalt hear tell concerning one of thy cities, which the LORD thy God giveth thee to dwell there, saying:

14. Certain base fellows are gone out from the midst of thee, and have drawn away the inhabitants of their city, saying: Let us go and serve other gods, which ye have not known;

15. Then shalt thou inquire, and make search, and ask diligently; and, behold, if it be truth, and the thing certain, that such abomination is wrought in the midst of thee;

16. Thou shalt surely smite the inhabitants of that city with the edge of the sword, destroying it utterly, and all that is therein and the cattle thereof, with the edge of the sword.

17. And thou shalt gather all the spoil of it into the midst of the broad place thereof, and shall burn with fire the city, and all the spoil thereof every whit, unto the LORD thy God; and it shall be a heap for ever; it shall not be built again.

18. And there shall cleave nought of the devoted thing to thy hand, that the LORD may turn from the fierceness of His anger, and show thee mercy, and have compassion upon thee, and multiply thee, as He hath sworn unto thy fathers;

19. When thou shalt hearken to the voice of the LORD thy God, to keep all His commandments which I command thee this day, to do that which is right in the eyes of the LORD thy God.

Chapter 14

1. Ye are the children of the LORD your God: ye shall not cut yourselves, nor make any baldness between your eyes for the dead.

2. For thou art a holy people unto the LORD thy God, and the LORD hath chosen thee to be His own treasure out of all peoples that are upon the face of the earth.

3. Thou shalt not eat any abominable thing.

4. These are the beasts which ye may eat: the ox, the sheep, and the goat,

5. The hart, and the gazelle, and the roebuck, and the wild goat, and the pygarg, and the antelope, and the mountain-sheep.

6. And every beast that parteth the hoof, and hath the hoof wholly cloven in two, and cheweth the cud, among the beasts, that ye may eat.

7. Nevertheless, these ye shall not eat of them that only chew the cud, or of them that only have the hoof cloven: the camel, and the hare, and the rock-badger, because they chew the cud but part not the hoof, they are unclean unto you;

8. And the swine, because he parteth the hoof but cheweth not the cud, he is unclean unto you; of their flesh ye shall not eat, and their carcasses ye shall not touch.

9. These ye may eat of all that are in the waters: whatsoever hath fins and scales may ye eat;

10. And whatsoever hath not fins and scales ye shall not eat; it is unclean unto you.

11. Of all clean birds ye may eat.

12. But these are they of which ye shall not eat: the great vulture, and the bearded vulture, and the ospray;

13. And the glede, and the falcon, and the kite after its kinds;

14. And every raven after its kinds;

15. And the ostrich, and the night-hawk, and the sea-mew, and the hawk after its kinds;

16. The little owl, and the great owl, and the horned owl;

17. And the pelican, and the carrion-vulture, and the cormorant;

18. And the stork, and the heron after its kinds, and the hoopoe, and the bat.

19. And all winged swarming things are unclean unto you; they shall not be eaten.

20. Of all clean winged things ye may eat.

21. Ye shall not eat of any thing that dieth of itself; thou mayest give it unto the stranger that is within thy gates, that he may eat it; or thou mayest sell it unto a foreigner; for thou art a holy people unto the LORD thy God. Thou shalt not seethe a kid in its mother's milk.

22. Thou shalt surely tithe all the increase of thy seed, that which is brought forth in the field year by year.

23. And thou shalt eat before the LORD thy God, in the place which He shall choose to cause His name to dwell there, the tithe of thy corn, of thy wine, and of thine oil, and the firstlings of thy herd and of thy flock; that thou mayest learn to fear the LORD thy God always.

24. And if the way be too long for thee, so that thou art not able to carry it, because the place is too far from thee, which the LORD thy God shall choose to set His name there, when the LORD thy God shall bless thee;

25. Then shalt thou turn it into money, and bind up the money in thy hand, and shalt go unto the place which the LORD thy God shall choose.

26. And thou shalt bestow the money for whatsoever thy soul desireth, for oxen, or for sheep, or for wine, or for strong drink, or for whatsoever thy soul asketh of thee; and thou shalt eat there before the LORD thy God, and thou shalt rejoice, thou and thy household.

27. And the Levite that is within thy gates, thou shalt not forsake him; for he hath no portion nor inheritance with thee.

28. At the end of every three years, even in the same year, thou shalt bring forth all the tithe of thine increase, and shall lay it up within thy gates.

29. And the Levite, because he hath no portion nor inheritance with thee, and the stranger, and the fatherless, and the widow, that are within thy gates, shall come, and shall eat and be satisfied; that the

LORD thy God may bless thee in all the work of thy hand which thou doest.

Chapter 15

1. At the end of every seven years, thou shalt make a release.

2. And this is the manner of the release: every creditor shall release that which he hath lent unto his neighbour; he shall not exact it of his neighbour and his brother; because the LORD'S release hath been proclaimed.

3. Of a foreigner thou mayest exact it; but whatsoever of thine is with thy brother thy hand shall release.

4. Howbeit there shall be no needy among you-for the LORD will surely bless thee in the land which the LORD thy God giveth thee for an inheritance to possess it.

5. If only thou diligently hearken unto the voice of the LORD thy God, to observe to do all this commandment which I command thee this day.

6. For the LORD thy God will bless thee, as He promised thee; and thou shalt lend unto many nations, but thou shalt not borrow; and thou shalt rule over many nations, but they shall not rule over thee.

7. If there be among you a needy man, one of thy brethren, within any of thy gates, in thy land which the LORD thy God giveth thee, thou shalt not harden thy heart, nor shut thy hand from thy needy brother;

8. But thou shalt surely open thy hand unto him, and

shalt surely lend him sufficient for his need in that which he wanteth.

9. Beware that there be not a base thought in thy heart, saying: The seventh year, the year of release, is at hand; and thine eye be evil against thy needy brother, and thou give him nought; and he cry unto the LORD against thee, and it be sin in thee.

10. Thou shalt surely give him, and thy heart shall not be grieved when thou givest unto him; because that for this thing the LORD thy God will bless thee in all thy work, and in all that thou puttest thy hand unto.

11. For the poor shall never cease out of the land; therefore, I command thee, saying: Thou shalt surely open thy hand unto thy poor and needy brother, in thy land.

12. If thy brother, a Hebrew man, or a Hebrew woman, be sold unto thee, he shall serve thee six years; and in the seventh year thou shalt let him go free from thee.

13. And when thou lettest him go free from thee, thou shalt not let him go empty;

14. Thou shalt furnish him liberally out of thy flock, and out of thy threshing-floor, and out of thy winepress; of that wherewith the LORD thy God hath blessed thee thou shalt give unto him.

15. And thou shalt remember that thou wast a bondman in the land of Egypt, and the LORD thy God redeemed thee; therefore, I command thee this thing to-day.

16. And it shall be, if he say unto thee: I will not go out from thee; because he loveth thee and thy house, because he fareth well with thee;

17. Then thou shalt take an awl, and thrust it through his ear and into the door, and he shall be thy bondman for ever. And also, unto thy bondwoman thou shalt do likewise.

18. It shall not seem hard unto thee, when thou lettest him go free from thee; for to the double of the hire of a hireling hath he served thee six years; and the LORD thy God will bless thee in all that thou doest.

19. All the firstling males that are born of thy herd and of thy flock thou shalt sanctify unto the LORD thy God; thou shalt do no work with the firstling of thine ox, nor shear the firstling of thy flock.

20. Thou shalt eat it before the LORD thy God year by year in the place which the LORD shall choose, thou and thy household.

21. And if there be any blemish therein, lameness, or blindness, any ill blemish whatsoever, thou shalt not sacrifice it unto the LORD thy God.

22. Thou shalt eat it within thy gates; the unclean and the clean may eat it alike, as the gazelle, and as the hart.

23. Only thou shalt not eat the blood thereof; thou shalt pour it out upon the ground as water.

Chapter 16

1. Observe the month of Abib, and keep the Passover

unto the LORD thy God; for in the month of Abib the LORD thy God brought thee forth out of Egypt by night.

2. And thou shalt sacrifice the Passover-offering unto the LORD thy God, of the flock and the herd, in the place which the LORD shall choose to cause His name to dwell there.

3. Thou shalt eat no leavened bread with it; seven days shalt thou eat unleavened bread therewith, even the bread of affliction; for in haste didst thou come forth out of the land of Egypt; that thou mayest remember the day when thou camest forth out of the land of Egypt all the days of thy life.

4. And there shall be no leaven seen with thee in all thy borders seven days; neither shall any of the flesh, which thou sacrificest the first day at even, remain all night until the morning.

5. Thou mayest not sacrifice the Passover-offering within any of thy gates, which the LORD thy God giveth thee;

6. But at the place which the LORD thy God shall choose to cause His name to dwell in, there thou shalt sacrifice the Passover-offering at even, at the going down of the sun, at the season that thou camest forth out of Egypt.

7. And thou shalt roast and eat it in the place which the LORD thy God shall choose; and thou shalt turn in the morning, and go unto thy tents.

8. Six days thou shalt eat unleavened bread; and on

the seventh day shall be a solemn assembly to the LORD thy God; thou shalt do no work therein.

9. Seven weeks shalt thou number unto thee; from the time the sickle is first put to the standing corn shalt thou begin to number seven weeks.

10. And thou shalt keep the feast of weeks unto the LORD thy God after the measure of the freewill-offering of thy hand, which thou shalt give, according as the LORD thy God blesseth thee.

11. And thou shalt rejoice before the LORD thy God, thou, and thy son, and thy daughter, and thy man-servant, and thy maid-servant, and the Levite that is within they gates, and the stranger, and the fatherless, and the widow, that are in the midst of thee, in the place which the LORD thy God shall choose to cause His name to dwell there.

12. And thou shalt remember that thou wast a bondman in Egypt; and thou shalt observe and do these statutes.

13. Thou shalt keep the feast of tabernacles seven days, after that thou hast gathered in from thy threshing-floor and from thy winepress.

14. And thou shalt rejoice in thy feast, thou, and thy son, and thy daughter, and thy man-servant, and thy maid-servant, and the Levite, and the stranger, and the fatherless, and the widow, that are within thy gates.

15. Seven days shalt thou keep a feast unto the LORD thy God in the place which the LORD shall choose;

because the LORD thy God shall bless thee in all thine increase, and in all the work of thy hands, and thou shalt be altogether joyful.

16. Three times in a year shall all thy males appear before the LORD thy God in the place which He shall choose; on the feast of unleavened bread, and on the feast of weeks, and on the feast of tabernacles; and they shall not appear before the LORD empty;

17. Every man shall give as he is able, according to the blessing of the LORD thy God which He hath given thee.

Shoftim

18. Judges and officers shalt thou make thee in all thy gates, which the LORD thy God giveth thee, tribe by tribe; and they shall judge the people with righteous judgment.

19. Thou shalt not wrest judgment; thou shalt not respect persons; neither shalt thou take a gift; for a gift doth blind the eyes of the wise, and pervert the words of the righteous.

20. Justice, justice shalt thou follow, that thou mayest live, and inherit the land which the LORD thy God giveth thee.

21. Thou shalt not plant thee an Asherah of any kind of tree beside the altar of the LORD thy God, which thou shalt make thee.

22. Neither shalt thou set thee up a pillar, which the

LORD thy God hateth.

Chapter 17

1. Thou shalt not sacrifice unto the LORD thy God an ox, or a sheep, wherein is a blemish, even any evil thing; for that is an abomination unto the LORD thy God.

2. If there be found in the midst of thee, within any of thy gates which the LORD thy God giveth thee, man or woman, that doeth that which is evil in the sight of the LORD thy God, in transgressing His covenant,

3. And hath gone and served other gods, and worshipped them, or the sun, or the moon, or any of the host of heaven, which I have commanded not;

4. And it be told thee, and thou hear it, then shalt thou inquire diligently, and, behold, if it be true, and the thing certain, that such abomination is wrought in Israel;

5. Then shalt thou bring forth that man or that woman, who have done this evil thing, unto thy gates, even the man or the woman; and thou shalt stone them with stones, that they die.

6. At the mouth of two witnesses, or three witnesses, shall he that is to die be put to death; at the mouth of one witness, he shall not be put to death.

7. The hand of the witnesses shall be first upon him to put him to death, and afterward the hand of all the people. So, thou shalt put away the evil from the midst of thee.

8. If there arise a matter too hard for thee in judgment, between blood and blood, between plea and plea, and between stroke and stroke, even matters of controversy within thy gates; then shalt thou arise, and get thee up unto the place which the LORD thy God shall choose.

9. And thou shall come unto the priests the Levites, and unto the judge that shall be in those days; and thou shalt inquire; and they shall declare unto thee the sentence of judgment.

10. And thou shalt do according to the tenor of the sentence, which they shall declare unto thee from that place which the LORD shall choose; and thou shalt observe to do according to all that they shall teach thee.

11. According to the law which they shall teach thee, and according to the judgment which they shall tell thee, thou shalt do; thou shalt not turn aside from the sentence which they shall declare unto thee, to the right hand, nor to the left.

12. And the man that doeth presumptuously, in not hearkening unto the priest that standeth to minister there before the LORD thy God, or unto the judge, even that man shall die; and thou shalt exterminate the evil from Israel.

13. And all the people shall hear, and fear, and do no more presumptuously.

14. When thou art come unto the land which the LORD thy God giveth thee, and shalt possess it, and shalt dwell therein; and shalt say: I will set a king over me, like all the nations that are round about me;

15. Thou shalt in any wise set him king over thee, whom the LORD thy God shall choose; one from among thy brethren shalt thou set king over thee; thou mayest not put a foreigner over thee, who is not thy brother.

16. Only he shall not multiply horses to himself, nor cause the people to return to Egypt, to the end that he should multiply horses; forasmuch as the LORD hath said unto you: Ye shall henceforth return no more that way.

17. Neither shall he multiply wives to himself, that his heart turn not away; neither shall he greatly multiply to himself silver and gold.

18. And it shall be, when he sitteth upon the throne of his kingdom, that he shall write him a copy of this law in a book, out of that which is before the priests the Levites.

19. And it shall be with him, and he shall read therein all the days of his life; that he may learn to fear the LORD his God, to keep all the words of this law and these statutes, to do them;

20. That his heart be not lifted up above his brethren, and that he turn not aside from the commandment, to the right hand, or to the left; to the end that he may prolong his days in his kingdom, he and his children, in the midst of Israel.

Chapter 18

1. The priests the Levites, even all the tribe of Levi, shall have no portion nor inheritance with Israel; they shall eat the offerings of the LORD made by fire, and His inheritance.

2. And they shall have no inheritance among their brethren; the LORD is their inheritance, as He hath spoken unto them.

3. And this shall be the priests' due from the people, from them that offer a sacrifice, whether it be ox or sheep, that they shall give unto the priest the shoulder, and the two cheeks, and the maw.

4. The first-fruits of thy corn, of thy wine, and of thine oil, and the first of the fleece of thy sheep, shalt thou give him.

5. For the LORD thy God hath chosen him out of all thy tribes, to stand to minister in the name of the LORD, him and his sons for ever.

6. And if a Levite come from any of thy gates out of all Israel, where he sojourneth, and come with all the desire of his soul unto the place which the LORD shall choose;

7. Then he shall minister in the name of the LORD his God, as all his brethren the Levites do, who stand there before the LORD.

8. They shall have like portions to eat, beside that which is his due according to the fathers' houses.

9. When thou art come into the land which the LORD thy God giveth thee, thou shalt not learn to do after the abominations of those nations.

10. There shall not be found among you any one that maketh his son or his daughter to pass through the fire, one that useth divination, a soothsayer, or an enchanter, or a sorcerer,

11. Or a charmer, or one that consulteth a ghost or a familiar spirit, or a necromancer.

12. For whosoever doeth these things is an abomination unto the LORD; and because of these abominations the LORD thy God is driving them out from before thee.

13. Thou shalt be whole-hearted with the LORD thy God.

14. For these nations, that thou art to dispossess, hearken unto soothsayers, and unto diviners; but as for thee, the LORD thy God hath not suffered thee so to do.

15. A prophet will the LORD thy God raise up unto thee, from the midst of thee, of thy brethren, like unto me; unto him ye shall hearken;

16. According to all that thou didst desire of the LORD thy God in Horeb in the day of the assembly, saying: Let me not hear again the voice of the LORD my God, neither let me see this great fire any more, that I die not.

17. And the LORD said unto me: They have well said that which they have spoken.

18. I will raise them up a prophet from among their brethren, like unto thee; and I will put My words in his mouth, and he shall speak unto them all that I shall command him.

19. And it shall come to pass, that whosoever will not hearken unto My words which he shall speak in My name, I will require it of him.

20. But the prophet, that shall speak a word presumptuously in My name, which I have not commanded him to speak, or that shall speak in the name of other gods, that same prophet shall die.

21. And if thou say in thy heart: How shall we know the word which the LORD hath not spoken?

22. When a prophet speaketh in the name of the LORD, if the thing follow not, nor come to pass, that is the thing which the LORD hath not spoken; the prophet hath spoken it presumptuously, thou shalt not be afraid of him.

Chapter 19

1. When the LORD thy God shall cut off the nations, whose land the LORD thy God giveth thee, and thou dost succeed them, and dwell in their cities, and in their houses;

2. Thou shalt separate three cities for thee in the midst of thy land, which the LORD thy GOD giveth thee to possess it.

3. Thou shalt prepare thee the way, and divide the borders of thy land, which the LORD thy God causeth thee to inherit, into three parts, that every manslayer may flee thither.

4. And this is the case of the manslayer, that shall flee thither and live: whoso killeth his neighbour unawares, and hated him not in time past;

5. As when a man goeth into the forest with his neighbour to hew wood, and his hand fetcheth a stroke with the axe to cut down the tree, and the head slippeth from the helve, and lighteth upon his neighbour, that he die; he shall flee unto one of these cities and live;

6. Lest the avenger of blood pursue the manslayer, while his heart is hot, and overtake him, because the way is long, and smite him mortally; whereas he was not deserving of death, inasmuch as he hated him not in time past.

7. Wherefore I command thee, saying: Thou shalt separate three cities for thee.

8. And if the LORD thy God enlarge thy border, as He hath sworn unto thy fathers, and give thee all the land which He promised to give unto thy fathers.

9. If thou shalt keep all this commandment to do it, which I command thee this day, to love the LORD thy God, and to walk ever in His ways-then shalt thou add three cities more for thee, beside these three;

10. That innocent blood be not shed in the midst of thy land, which the LORD thy God giveth thee for an inheritance, and so blood be upon thee.

11. But if any man hate his neighbour, and lie in wait for him, and rise up against him, and smite him mortally that he die; and he flee into one of these cities;

12. Then the elders of his city shall send and fetch him thence, and deliver him into the hand of the avenger of blood, that he may die.

13. Thine eye shall not pity him, but thou shalt put away the blood of the innocent from Israel, that it may go well with thee.

14. Thou shalt not remove thy neighbour's landmark, which they of old time have set, in thine inheritance which thou shalt inherit, in the land that the LORD thy God giveth thee to possess it.

15. One witness shall not rise up against a man for any iniquity, or for any sin, in any sin that he sinneth; at the mouth of two witnesses, or at the mouth of three witnesses, shall a matter be established.

16. If an unrighteous witness rise up against any man to bear perverted witness against him;

17. Then both the men, between whom the controversy is, shall stand before the LORD, before the priests and the judges that shall be in those days.

18. And the judges shall inquire diligently; and, behold, if the witness be a false witness, and hath testified falsely against his brother;

19. Then shall ye do unto him, as he had purposed to do unto his brother; so shalt thou put away the evil from the midst of thee.

20. And those that remain shall hear, and fear, and shall henceforth commit no more any such evil in the midst of thee.

21. And thine eye shall not pity: life for life, eye for eye, tooth for tooth, hand for hand, foot for foot.

Chapter 20

1. When thou goest forth to battle against thine enemies, and seest horses, and chariots, and a people more than thou, thou shalt not be afraid of them; for the LORD thy God is with thee, who brought thee up out of the land of Egypt.

2. And it shall be, when ye draw nigh unto the battle, that the priest shall approach and speak unto the people,

3. And shall say unto them: Hear, O Israel, ye draw nigh this day unto battle against your enemies; let not your heart faint; fear not, nor be alarmed, neither be ye affrighted at them;

4. For the LORD your God is He that goeth with you, to fight for you against your enemies, to save you.

5. And the officers shall speak unto the people, saying: What man is there that hath built a new house, and hath not dedicated it? let him go and return to his house, lest he die in the battle, and another man dedicate it.

6. And what man is there that hath planted a vineyard, and hath not used the fruit thereof? let him go and return unto his house, lest he die in the battle, and another man use the fruit thereof.

7. And what man is there that hath betrothed a wife, and hath not taken her? let him go and return unto his house, lest he die in the battle, and another man take her.

8. And the officers shall speak further unto the people, and they shall say: What man is there that is fearful and faint-hearted? let him go and return unto his house, lest his brethren's heart melt as his heart.

9. And it shall be, when the officers have made an end of speaking unto the people, that captains of hosts shall be appointed at the head of the people.

10. When thou drawest nigh unto a city to fight against it, then proclaim peace unto it.

11. And it shall be, if it make thee answer of peace, and open unto thee, then it shall be, that all the people that are found therein shall become tributary unto thee, and shall serve thee.

12. And if it will make no peace with thee, but will make war against thee, then thou shalt besiege it.

13. And when the LORD thy God delivereth it into thy hand, thou shalt smite every male thereof with the edge of the sword;

14. But the women, and the little ones, and the cattle, and all that is in the city, even all the spoil thereof, shalt thou take for a prey unto thyself; and thou shalt eat the spoil of thine enemies, which the LORD thy God hath given thee.

15. Thus, shalt thou do unto all the cities which are very far off from thee, which are not of the cities of these nations.

16. Howbeit of the cities of these peoples, that the

LORD thy God giveth thee for an inheritance, thou shalt save alive nothing that breatheth,

17. But thou shalt utterly destroy them: the Hittite, and the Amorite, the Canaanite, and the Perizzite, the Hivite, and the Jebusite; as the LORD thy God hath commanded thee;

18. That they teach you not to do after all their abominations, which they have done unto their gods, and so ye sin against the LORD your God.

19. When thou shalt besiege a city a long time, in making war against it to take it, thou shalt not destroy the trees thereof by wielding an axe against them; for thou mayest eat of them, but thou shalt not cut them down; for is the tree of the field man, that it should be besieged of thee?

20. Only the trees of which thou knowest that they are not trees for food, them thou mayest destroy and cut down, that thou mayest build bulwarks against the city that maketh war with thee, until it fall.

Chapter 21

1. If one be found slain in the land which the LORD thy God giveth thee to possess it, lying in the field, and it be not known who hath smitten him;

2. Then thy elders and thy judges shall come forth, and they shall measure unto the cities which are round about him that is slain.

3. And it shall be, that the city which is nearest unto the slain man, even the elders of that city shall take a heifer of the herd, which hath not been wrought with, and which hath not drawn in the yoke.

4. And the elders of that city shall bring down the heifer unto a rough valley, which may neither be plowed nor sown, and shall break the heifer's neck there in the valley.

5. And the priests the sons of Levi shall come near-for them the LORD thy God hath chosen to minister unto Him, and to bless in the name of the LORD; and according to their word shall every controversy and every stroke be.

6. And all the elders of that city, who are nearest unto the slain man, shall wash their hands over the heifer whose neck was broken in the valley.

7. And they shall speak and say: Our hands have not shed this blood, neither have our eyes seen it.

8. Forgive, O LORD; Thy people Israel, whom Thou hast redeemed, and suffer not innocent blood to remain in the midst of Thy people Israel. And the blood shall be forgiven them.

9. So shalt thou put away the innocent blood from the midst of thee, when thou shalt do that which is right in the eyes of the LORD.

Ki Teitzei

10. When thou goest forth to battle against thine enemies, and the LORD thy God delivereth them into thy hands, and thou carriest them away captive,

11. And seest among the captives a woman of goodly form, and thou hast a desire unto her, and wouldest take her to thee to wife;

12. Then thou shalt bring her home to thy house; and she shall shave her head, and pare her nails;

13. And she shall put the raiment of her captivity from off her, and shall remain in thy house, and bewail her father and her mother a full month; and after that thou mayest go in unto her, and be her husband, and she shall be thy wife.

14. And it shall be, if thou have no delight in her, then thou shalt let her go whither she will; but thou shalt not sell her at all for money, thou shalt not deal with her as a slave, because thou hast humbled her.

15. If a man have two wives, the one beloved, and the other hated, and they have borne him children, both the beloved and the hated; and if the first-born son be hers that was hated;

16. Then it shall be, in the day that he causeth his sons to inherit that which he hath, that he may not make the son of the beloved the first-born before the son of the hated, who is the first-born;

17. But he shall acknowledge the first-born, the son of the hated, by giving him a double portion of all that he hath; for he is the first-fruits of his strength, the right of the first-born is his.

18. If a man have a stubborn and rebellious son, that will not hearken to the voice of his father, or the voice of his mother, and though they chasten him, will not hearken unto them;

19. Then shall his father and his mother lay hold on him, and bring him out unto the elders of his city, and unto the gate of his place;

20. And they shall say unto the elders of his city: This our son is stubborn and rebellious, he doth not hearken to our voice; he is a glutton, and a drunkard.

21. And all the men of his city shall stone him with stones, that he die; so shalt thou put away the evil from the midst of thee; and all Israel shall hear, and fear.

22. And if a man have committed a sin worthy of death, and he be put to death, and thou hang him on a tree;

23. His body shall not remain all night upon the tree, but thou shalt surely bury him the same day; for he that is hanged is a reproach unto God; that thou defile not thy land which the LORD thy God giveth thee for an inheritance.

Chapter 22

1. Thou shalt not see thy brother's ox or his sheep driven away, and hide thyself from them; thou shalt surely bring them back unto thy brother.

2. And if thy brother be not nigh unto thee, and thou know him not, then thou shalt bring it home to thy house, and it shall be with thee until thy brother require it, and thou shalt restore it to him.

3. And so shalt thou do with his ass; and so shalt thou

do with his garment; and so shalt thou do with every lost thing of thy brother's, which he hath lost, and thou hast found; thou mayest not hide thyself.

4. Thou shalt not see thy brother's ass or his ox fallen down by the way, and hide thyself from them; thou shalt surely help him to lift them up again.

5. A woman shall not wear that which pertaineth unto a man, neither shall a man put on a woman's garment; for whosoever doeth these things is an abomination unto the LORD thy God.

6. If a bird's nest chance to be before thee in the way, in any tree or on the ground, with young ones or eggs, and the dam sitting upon the young, or upon the eggs, thou shalt not take the dam with the young;

7. Thou shalt in any wise let the dam go, but the young thou mayest take unto thyself; that it may be well with thee, and that thou mayest prolong thy days.

8. When thou buildest a new house, then thou shalt make a parapet for thy roof, that thou bring not blood upon thy house, if any man fall from thence.

9. Thou shalt not sow thy vineyard with two kinds of seed; lest the fulness of the seed which thou hast sown be forfeited together with the increase of the vineyard.

10. Thou shalt not plow with an ox and an ass together.

11. Thou shalt not wear a mingled stuff, wool and linen together.

12. Thou shalt make thee twisted cords upon the four

corners of thy covering, wherewith thou coverest thyself.

13. If any man take a wife, and go in unto her, and hate her,

14. And lay wanton charges against her, and bring up an evil name upon her, and say: I took this woman, and when I came nigh to her, I found not in her the tokens of virginity;

15. Then shall the father of the damsel, and her mother, take and bring forth the tokens of the damsel's virginity unto the elders of the city in the gate.

16. And the damsel's father shall say unto the elders: I gave my daughter unto this man to wife, and he hateth her;

17. And, lo, he hath laid wanton charges, saying: I found not in thy daughter the tokens of virginity; and yet these are the tokens of my daughter's virginity. And they shall spread the garment before the elders of the city.

18. And the elders of that city shall take the man and chastise him.

19. And they shall fine him a hundred shekels of silver, and give them unto the father of the damsel, because he hath brought up an evil name upon a virgin of Israel; and she shall be his wife; he may not put her away all his days.

20. But if this thing be true, that the tokens of virginity were not found in the damsel;

21. Then they shall bring out the damsel to the door of her father's house, and the men of her city shall stone her with stones that she die; because she hath wrought a wanton deed in Israel, to play the harlot in her father's house; so shalt thou put away the evil from the midst of thee.

22. If a man be found lying with a woman married to a husband, then they shall both of them die, the man that lay with the woman, and the woman; so shalt thou put away the evil from Israel.

23. If there be a damsel that is a virgin betrothed unto a man, and a man find her in the city, and lie with her;

24. Then ye shall bring them both out unto the gate of that city, and ye shall stone them with stones that they die: the damsel, because she cried not, being in the city; and the man, because he hath humbled his neighbour's wife; so, thou shalt put away the evil from the midst of thee.

25. But if the man find the damsel that is betrothed in the field, and the man take hold of her, and lie with her; then the man only that lay with her shall die.

26. But unto the damsel thou shalt do nothing; there is in the damsel no sin worthy of death; for as when a man riseth against his neighbour, and slayeth him, even so is this matter.

27. For he found her in the field; the betrothed damsel cried, and there was none to save her.

28. If a man find a damsel that is a virgin, that is not betrothed, and lay hold on her, and lie with her, and they be found;

29. Then the man that lay with her shall give unto the damsel's father fifty shekels of silver, and she shall be his wife, because he hath humbled her; he may not put her away all his days.

Chapter 23

1. A man shall not take his father's wife, and shall not uncover his father's skirt.

2. He that is crushed or maimed in his privy parts shall not enter into the assembly of the LORD.

3. A bastard shall not enter into the assembly of the LORD; even to the tenth generation shall none of his enter into the assembly of the LORD.

4. An Ammonite or a Moabite shall not enter into the assembly of the LORD; even to the tenth generation shall none of them enter into the assembly of the LORD for ever;

5. Because they met you not with bread and with water in the way, when ye came forth out of Egypt; and because they hired against thee Balaam the son of Beor from Pethor of Aram-naharaim, to curse thee.

6. Nevertheless, the LORD thy God would not hearken unto Balaam; but the LORD thy God turned the curse into a blessing unto thee, because the LORD thy God loved thee.

7. Thou shalt not seek their peace nor their prosperity all thy days for ever.

8. Thou shalt not abhor an Edomite, for he is thy

brother; thou shalt not abhor an Egyptian, because thou wast a stranger in his land.

9. The children of the third generation that are born unto them may enter into the assembly of the LORD.

10. When thou goest forth in camp against thine enemies, then thou shalt keep thee from every evil thing.

11. If there be among you any man, that is not clean by reason of that which chanceth him by night, then shall he go abroad out of the camp, he shall not come within the camp.

12. But it shall be, when evening cometh on, he shall bathe himself in water; and when the sun is down, he may come within the camp.

13. Thou shalt have a place also without the camp, whither thou shalt go forth abroad.

14. With your gear you shall have a spike, and when you have squatted you shall dig a hole with it and cover up your excrement.

15. For the LORD thy God walketh in the midst of thy camp, to deliver thee, and to give up thine enemies before thee; therefore, shall thy camp be holy; that He see no unseemly thing in thee, and turn away from thee.

16. Thou shalt not deliver unto his master a bondman that is escaped from his master unto thee;

17. He shall dwell with thee, in the midst of thee, in the place which he shall choose within one of thy gates, where it liketh him best; thou shalt not wrong him.

18. There shall be no harlot of the daughters of Israel, neither shall there be a sodomite of the sons of Israel.

19. Thou shalt not bring the hire of a harlot, or the price of a dog, into the house of the LORD thy God for any vow; for even both these are an abomination unto the LORD thy God.

20. Thou shalt not lend upon interest to thy brother: interest of money, interest of victuals, interest of any thing that is lent upon interest.

21. Unto a foreigner thou mayest lend upon interest; but unto thy brother thou shalt not lend upon interest; that the LORD thy God may bless thee in all that thou puttest thy hand unto, in the land whither thou goest in to possess it.

22. When thou shalt vow a vow unto the LORD thy God, thou shalt not be slack to pay it; for the LORD thy God will surely require it of thee; and it will be sin in thee.

23. But if thou shalt forbear to vow, it shall be no sin in thee.

24. That which is gone out of thy lips thou shalt observe and do; according as thou hast vowed freely unto the LORD thy God, even that which thou hast promised with thy mouth.

25. When thou comest into thy neighbour's vineyard, then thou mayest eat grapes until thou have enough at thine own pleasure; but thou shalt not put any in thy vessel.

26. When thou comest into thy neighbour's standing corn, then thou mayest pluck ears with thy hand; but thou shalt not move a sickle unto thy neighbour's standing corn.

Chapter 24

1. When a man taketh a wife, and marrieth her, then it cometh to pass, if she find no favour in his eyes, because he hath found some unseemly thing in her, that he writeth her a bill of divorcement, and giveth it in her hand, and sendeth her out of his house,
2. And she departeth out of his house, and goeth and becometh another man's wife,
3. And the latter husband hateth her, and writeth her a bill of divorcement, and giveth it in her hand, and sendeth her out of his house; or if the latter husband die, who took her to be his wife;
4. Her former husband, who sent her away, may not take her again to be his wife, after that she is defiled; for that is abomination before the LORD; and thou shalt not cause the land to sin, which the LORD thy God giveth thee for an inheritance.
5. When a man taketh a new wife, he shall not go out in the host, neither shall he be charged with any business; he shall be free for his house one year, and shall cheer his wife whom he hath taken.
6. No man shall take the mill or the upper millstone to pledge; for he taketh a man's life to pledge.
7. If a man be found stealing any of his brethren of

the children of Israel, and he deal with him as a slave, and sell him; then that thief shall die; so shalt thou put away the evil from the midst of thee.

8. Take heed in the plague of leprosy, that thou observe diligently, and do according to all that the priests the Levites shall teach you, as I commanded them, so ye shall observe to do.

9. Remember what the LORD thy God did unto Miriam, by the way as ye came forth out of Egypt.

10. When thou dost lend thy neighbour any manner of loan, thou shalt not go into his house to fetch his pledge.

11. Thou shalt stand without, and the man to whom thou dost lend shall bring forth the pledge without unto thee.

12. And if he be a poor man, thou shalt not sleep with his pledge;

13. Thou shalt surely restore to him the pledge when the sun goeth down, that he may sleep in his garment, and bless thee; and it shall be righteousness unto thee before the LORD thy God.

14. Thou shalt not oppress a hired servant that is poor and needy, whether he be of thy brethren, or of thy strangers that are in thy land within thy gates.

15. In the same day thou shalt give him his hire, neither shall the sun go down upon it; for he is poor, and setteth his heart upon it: lest he cry against thee unto the LORD and it be sin in thee.

16. The fathers shall not be put to death for the

children, neither shall the children be put to death for the fathers; every man shall be put to death for his own sin.

17. Thou shalt not pervert the justice due to the stranger, or to the fatherless; nor take the widow's raiment to pledge.

18. But thou shalt remember that thou wast a bondman in Egypt, and the LORD thy God redeemed thee thence; therefore, I command thee to do this thing.

19. When thou reapest thy harvest in thy field, and hast forgot a sheaf in the field, thou shalt not go back to fetch it; it shall be for the stranger, for the fatherless, and for the widow; that the LORD thy God may bless thee in all the work of thy hands.

20. When thou beatest thine olive-tree, thou shalt not go over the boughs again; it shall be for the stranger, for the fatherless, and for the widow.

21. When thou gatherest the grapes of thy vineyard, thou shalt not glean it after thee; it shall be for the stranger, for the fatherless, and for the widow.

22. And thou shalt remember that thou wast a bondman in the land of Egypt; therefore, I command thee to do this thing.

Chapter 25

1. If there be a controversy between men, and they come unto judgment, and the judges judge them, by justifying the righteous, and condemning the wicked,

2. Then it shall be, if the wicked man deserve to be beaten, that the judge shall cause him to lie down, and to be beaten before his face, according to the measure of his wickedness, by number.

3. Forty stripes he may give him, he shall not exceed; lest, if he should exceed, and beat him above these with many stripes, then thy brother should be dishonoured before thine eyes.

4. Thou shalt not muzzle the ox when he treadeth out the corn.

5. If brethren dwell together, and one of them die, and have no child, the wife of the dead shall not be married abroad unto one not of his kin; her husband's brother shall go in unto her, and take her to him to wife, and perform the duty of a husband's brother unto her.

6. And it shall be, that the first-born that she beareth shall succeed in the name of his brother that is dead, that his name be not blotted out of Israel.

7. And if the man like not to take his brother's wife, then his brother's wife shall go up to the gate unto the elders, and say: My husband's brother refuseth to raise up unto his brother a name in Israel; he will not perform the duty of a husband's brother unto me.

8. Then the elders of his city shall call him, and speak unto him; and if he stand, and say: I like not to take her;

9. Then shall his brother's wife draw nigh unto him in the presence of the elders, and loose his shoe from off his foot, and spit in his face; and she shall answer and say: So, shall it be done unto the man that doth not build up his brother's house.

10. And his name shall be called in Israel - The house of him that had his shoe loosed.

11. When men strive together one with another, and the wife of the one draweth near to deliver her husband out of the hand of him that smiteth him, and putteth forth her hand, and taketh him by the secrets;

12. Then thou shalt cut off her hand, thine eye shall have no pity.

13. Thou shalt not have in thy bag diverse weights, a great and a small.

14. Thou shalt not have in thy house diverse measures, a great and a small.

15. A perfect and just weight shalt thou have; a perfect and just measure shalt thou have; that thy days may be long upon the land which the LORD thy God giveth thee.

16. For all that do such things, even all that do unrighteously, are an abomination unto the LORD thy God.

17. Remember what Amalek did unto thee by the way as ye came forth out of Egypt;

18. How he met thee by the way, and smote the hindmost of thee, all that were enfeebled in thy rear, when thou wast faint and weary; and he feared not God.

19. Therefore, it shall be, when the LORD thy God

hath given, thee rest from all thine enemies round about, in the land which the LORD thy God giveth thee for an inheritance to possess it, that thou shalt blot out the remembrance of Amalek from under heaven; thou shalt not forget.

Ki Tavo

Chapter 26

1. And it shall be, when thou art come in unto the land which the LORD thy God giveth thee for an inheritance, and dost possess it, and dwell therein;

2. That thou shalt take of the first of all the fruit of the ground, which thou shalt bring in from thy land that the LORD thy God giveth thee; and thou shalt put it in a basket and shalt go unto the place which the LORD thy God shall choose to cause His name to dwell there.

3. And thou shalt come unto the priest that shall be in those days, and say unto him: I profess this day unto the LORD thy God, that I am come unto the land which the LORD swore unto our fathers to give us.

4. And the priest shall take the basket out of thy hand, and set it down before the altar of the LORD thy God.

5. And thou shalt speak and say before the LORD thy God: A wandering Aramean was my father, and he went down into Egypt, and sojourned there, few in number; and he became there a nation, great, mighty, and populous.

6. And the Egyptians dealt ill with us, and afflicted us, and laid upon us hard bondage.

7. And we cried unto the LORD, the God of our fathers, and the LORD heard our voice, and saw our affliction, and our toil, and our oppression.

8. And the LORD brought us forth out of Egypt with a mighty hand, and with an outstretched arm, and with great terribleness, and with signs, and with wonders.

9. And He hath brought us into this place, and hath given us this land, a land flowing with milk and honey.

10. And now, behold, I have brought the first of the fruit of the land, which Thou, O LORD, hast given me. And thou shalt set it down before the LORD thy God, and worship before the LORD thy God.

11. And thou shalt rejoice in all the good which the LORD thy God hath given unto thee, and unto thy house, thou, and the Levite, and the stranger that is in the midst of thee.

12. When thou hast made an end of tithing all the tithe of thine increase in the third year, which is the year of tithing, and hast given it unto the Levite, to the stranger, to the fatherless, and to the widow, that they may eat within thy gates, and be satisfied,

13. Then thou shalt say before the LORD thy God: I have put away the hallowed things out of my house, and also have given them unto the Levite, and unto the stranger, to the fatherless, and to the widow, according to all Thy commandment which Thou hast commanded me; I have not transgressed any of Thy commandments, neither have I forgotten them.

14. I have not eaten thereof in my mourning, neither have I put away thereof, being unclean, nor given thereof for the dead; I have hearkened to the voice of the LORD my God, I have done according to all that Thou hast commanded me.

15. Look forth from Thy holy habitation, from heaven, and bless Thy people Israel, and the land which Thou hast given us, as Thou didst swear unto our fathers, a land flowing with milk and honey.

16. This day the LORD thy God commandeth thee to do these statutes and ordinances; thou shalt therefore observe and do them with all thy heart, and with all thy soul.

17. Thou hast avouched the LORD this day to be thy God, and that thou wouldest walk in His ways, and keep His statutes, and His commandments, and His ordinances, and hearken unto His voice.

18. And the LORD hath avouched thee this day to be His own treasure, as He hath promised thee, and that thou shouldest keep all His commandments;

19. And to make thee high above all nations that He hath made, in praise, and in name, and in glory; and that thou mayest be a holy people unto the LORD thy God, as He hath spoken.

Chapter 27

1. And Moses and the elders of Israel commanded the people, saying: Keep all the commandment which I command you this day.

2. And it shall be on the day when ye shall pass over the Jordan unto the land which the LORD thy God giveth thee, that thou shalt set thee up great stones, and plaster them with plaster.

3. And thou shalt write upon them all the words of this law, when thou art passed over; that thou mayest go in unto the land which the LORD thy God giveth thee, a land flowing with milk and honey, as the LORD, the God of thy fathers, hath promised thee.

4. And it shall be when ye are passed over the Jordan, that ye shall set up these stones, which I command you this day, in mount Ebal, and thou shalt plaster them with plaster.

5. And there shalt thou build an altar unto the LORD thy God, an altar of stones; thou shalt lift up no iron tool upon them.

6. Thou shalt build the altar of the LORD thy God of unhewn stones; and thou shalt offer burnt-offerings thereon unto the LORD thy God.

7. And thou shalt sacrifice peace-offerings, and shalt eat there; and thou shalt rejoice before the LORD thy God.

8. And thou shalt write upon the stones all the words of this law very plainly.

9. And Moses and the priests the Levites spoke unto

all Israel, saying: Keep silence, and hear, O Israel; this day thou art become a people unto the LORD thy God.

10. Thou shalt therefore hearken to the voice of the LORD thy God, and do His commandments and His statutes, which I command thee this day.

11. And Moses charged the people the same day, saying:

12. These shall stand upon mount Gerizim to bless the people, when ye are passed over the Jordan: Simeon, and Levi, and Judah, and Issachar, and Joseph, and Benjamin;

13. And these shall stand upon mount Ebal for the curse: Reuben, Gad, and Asher, and Zebulun, Dan, and Naphtali.

14. And the Levites shall speak, and say unto all the men of Israel with a loud voice:

15. Cursed be the man that maketh a graven or molten image, an abomination unto the LORD, the work of the hands of the craftsman, and setteth it up in secret. And all the people shall answer and say: Amen.

16. Cursed be he that dishonoureth his father or his mother. And all the people shall say: Amen.

17. Cursed be he that removeth his neighbour's landmark. And all the people shall say: Amen.

18. Cursed be he that maketh the blind to go astray in the way. And all the people shall say: Amen.

19. Cursed be he that perverteth the justice due to the stranger, fatherless, and widow. And all the people shall say: Amen.

20. Cursed be he that lieth with his father's wife; because he hath uncovered his father's skirt. And all the people shall say: Amen.

21. Cursed be he that lieth with any manner of beast. And all the people shall say: Amen.

22. Cursed be he that lieth with his sister, the daughter of his father, or the daughter of his mother. And all the people shall say: Amen.

23. Cursed be he that lieth with his mother-in-law. And all the people shall say: Amen.

24. Cursed be he that smiteth his neighbour in secret. And all the people shall say: Amen.

25. Cursed be he that taketh a bribe to slay an innocent person. And all the people shall say: Amen.

26. Cursed be he that confirmeth not the words of this law to do them. And all the people shall say: Amen.

Chapter 28

1. And it shall come to pass, if thou shalt hearken diligently unto the voice of the LORD thy God, to observe to do all His commandments which I command thee this day, that the LORD thy God will set thee on high above all the nations of the earth.

2. And all these blessings shall come upon thee, and overtake thee, if thou shalt hearken unto the voice of the LORD thy God.

3. Blessed shalt thou be in the city, and blessed shalt thou be in the field.

4. Blessed shall be the fruit of thy body, and the fruit of thy land, and the fruit of thy cattle, the increase of thy kine, and the young of thy flock.

5. Blessed shall be thy basket and thy kneading-trough.

6. Blessed shalt thou be when thou comest in, and blessed shalt thou be when thou goest out.

7. The LORD will cause thine enemies that rise up against thee to be smitten before thee; they shall come out against thee one way, and shall flee before thee seven ways.

8. The LORD will command the blessing with thee in thy barns, and in all that thou puttest thy hand unto; and He will bless thee in the land which the LORD thy God giveth thee.

9. The LORD will establish thee for a holy people unto Himself, as He hath sworn unto thee; if thou shalt keep the commandments of the LORD thy God, and walk in His ways.

10. And all the peoples of the earth shall see that the name of the LORD is called upon thee; and they shall be afraid of thee.

11. And the LORD will make thee over-abundant for good, in the fruit of thy body, and in the fruit of thy cattle, and in the fruit of thy land, in the land which the LORD swore unto thy fathers to give thee.

12. The LORD will open unto thee His good treasure the heaven to give the rain of thy land in its season, and to bless all the work of thy hand; and thou shalt lend unto many nations, but thou shalt not borrow.

13. And the LORD will make thee the head, and not the tail; and thou shalt be above only, and thou shalt not be beneath; if thou shalt hearken unto the commandments of the LORD thy God, which I command thee this day, to observe and to do them;

14. And shalt not turn aside from any of the words which I command you this day, to the right hand, or to the left, to go after other gods to serve them.

15. But it shall come to pass, if thou wilt not hearken unto the voice of the LORD thy God, to observe to do all His commandments and His statutes which I command thee this day; that all these curses shall come upon thee, and overtake thee.

16. Cursed shalt thou be in the city, and cursed shalt thou be in the field.

17. Cursed shall be thy basket and thy kneading-trough.

18. Cursed shall be the fruit of thy body, and the fruit of thy land, the increase of thy kine, and the young of thy flock.

19. Cursed shalt thou be when thou comest in, and cursed shalt thou be when thou goest out.

20. The LORD will send upon thee cursing, discomfiture, and rebuke, in all that thou puttest thy hand unto to do, until thou be destroyed, and until thou perish quickly; because of the evil of thy doings, whereby thou hast forsaken Me.

21. The LORD will make the pestilence cleave unto

thee, until He have consumed thee from off the land, whither thou goest in to possess it.

22. The LORD will smite thee with consumption, and with fever, and with inflammation, and with fiery heat, and with drought, and with blasting, and with mildew; and they shall pursue thee until thou perish.

23. And thy heaven that is over thy head shall be brass, and the earth that is under thee shall be iron.

24. The LORD will make the rain of thy land powder and dust; from heaven shall it come down upon thee, until thou be destroyed.

25. The LORD will cause thee to be smitten before thine enemies; thou shalt go out one way against them, and shalt flee seven ways before them; and thou shalt be a horror unto all the kingdoms of the earth.

26. And thy carcasses shall be food unto all fowls of the air, and unto the beasts of the earth, and there shall be none to frighten them away.

27. The LORD will smite thee with the boil of Egypt, and with the emerods, and with the scab, and with the itch, whereof thou canst not be healed.

28. The LORD will smite thee with madness, and with blindness, and with astonishment of heart.

29. And thou shalt grope at noonday, as the blind gropeth in darkness, and thou shalt not make thy ways prosperous; and thou shalt be only oppressed and robbed alway, and there shall be none to save thee.

30. Thou shalt betroth a wife, and another man shall lie with her; thou shalt build a house, and thou shalt not dwell therein; thou shalt plant a vineyard, and shalt not use the fruit thereof.

31. Thine ox shall be slain before thine eyes, and thou shalt not eat thereof; thine ass shall be violently taken away from before thy face, and shall not be restored to thee; thy sheep shall be given unto thine enemies; and thou shalt have none to save thee.

32. Thy sons and thy daughters shall be given unto another people, and thine eyes shall look, and fail with longing for them all the day; and there shall be nought in the power of thy hand.

33. The fruit of thy land, and all thy labours, shall a nation which thou knowest not eat up; and thou shalt be only oppressed and crushed away:

34. So that thou shalt be mad for the sight of thine eyes which thou shalt see.

35. The LORD will smite thee in the knees, and in the legs, with a sore boil, whereof thou canst not be healed, from the sole of thy foot unto the crown of thy head.

36. The LORD will bring thee, and thy king whom thou shalt set over thee, unto a nation that thou hast not known, thou nor thy fathers; and there shalt thou serve other gods, wood and stone.

37. And thou shalt become an astonishment, a proverb, and a byword, among all the peoples whither the LORD shall lead thee away.

38. Thou shalt carry much seed out into the field, and shalt gather little in; for the locust shall consume it.

39. Thou shalt plant vineyards and dress them, but thou shalt neither drink of the wine, nor gather the grapes; for the worm shall eat them.

40. Thou shalt have olive-trees throughout all thy borders, but thou shalt not anoint thyself with the oil; for thine olives shall drop off.

41. Thou shalt beget sons and daughters, but they shall not be thine; for they shall go into captivity.

42. All thy trees and the fruit of thy land shall the locust possess.

43. The stranger that is in the midst of thee shall mount up above thee higher and higher; and thou shalt come down lower and lower.

44. He shall lend to thee, and thou shalt not lend to him; he shall be the head, and thou shalt be the tail.

45. And all these curses shall come upon thee, and shall pursue thee, and overtake thee, till thou be destroyed; because thou didst not hearken unto the voice of the LORD thy God, to keep His commandments and His statutes which He commanded thee.

46. And they shall be upon thee for a sign and for a wonder, and upon thy seed for ever;

47. Because thou didst not serve the LORD thy God with joyfulness, and with gladness of heart, by reason of the abundance of all things;

48. Therefore, shalt thou serve thine enemy whom the LORD shall send against thee, in hunger, and in thirst, and in nakedness, and in want of all things; and he shall put a yoke of iron upon thy neck, until he have destroyed thee.

49. The LORD will bring a nation against thee from far, from the end of the earth, as the vulture swoopeth down; a nation whose tongue thou shalt not understand;

50. A nation of fierce countenance, that shall not regard the person of the old, nor show favour to the young.

51. And he shall eat the fruit of thy cattle, and the fruit of thy ground, until thou be destroyed; that also shall not leave thee corn, wine, or oil, the increase of thy kine, or the young of thy flock, until he have caused thee to perish.

52. And he shall besiege thee in all thy gates, until thy high and fortified walls come down, wherein thou didst trust, throughout all thy land; and he shall besiege thee in all thy gates throughout all thy land, which the LORD thy God hath given thee.

53. And thou shalt eat the fruit of thine own body, the flesh of thy sons and of thy daughters whom the LORD thy God hath given thee; in the siege and in the straitness, wherewith thine enemies shall straiten thee.

54. The man that is tender among you, and very delicate, his eye shall be evil against his brother, and against the wife of his bosom, and against the remnant of his children whom he hath remaining;

55. So that he will not give to any of them of the flesh of his children whom he shall eat, because he hath nothing left him; in the siege and in the straitness, wherewith thine enemy shall straiten thee in all thy gates.

56. The tender and delicate woman among you, who would not adventure to set the sole of her foot upon the ground for delicateness and tenderness, her eye shall be evil against the husband of her bosom, and against her son, and against her daughter;

57. And against her afterbirth that cometh out from between her feet, and against her children whom she shall bear; for she shall eat them for want of all things secretly; in the siege and in the straitness, wherewith thine enemy shall straiten thee in thy gates.

58. If thou wilt not observe to do all the words of this law that are written in this book, that thou mayest fear this glorious and awful Name, the LORD thy God;

59. Then the LORD will make thy plagues wonderful, and the plagues of thy seed, even great plagues, and of long continuance, and sore sicknesses, and of long continuance.

60. And He will bring back upon thee all the diseases of Egypt, which thou wast in dread of; and they shall cleave unto thee.

61. Also, every sickness, and every plague, which is not written in the book of this law, them will the LORD bring upon thee, until thou be destroyed.

62. And ye shall be left few in number, whereas ye were as the stars of heaven for multitude; because thou didst not hearken unto the voice of the LORD thy God.

63. And it shall come to pass, that as the LORD rejoiced over you to do you good, and to multiply you; so, the LORD will rejoice over you to cause you to perish, and to destroy you; and ye shall be plucked from off the land whither thou goest in to possess it.

64. And the LORD shall scatter thee among all peoples, from the one end of the earth even unto the other end of the earth; and there thou shalt serve other gods, which thou hast not known, thou nor thy fathers, even wood and stone.

65. And among these nations shalt thou have no repose, and there shall be no rest for the sole of thy foot; but the LORD shall give thee there a trembling heart, and failing of eyes, and languishing of soul.

66. And thy life shall hang in doubt before thee; and thou shalt fear night and day, and shalt have no assurance of thy life.

67. In the morning thou shalt say: Would it were even! and at even thou shalt say: Would it were morning! for the fear of thy heart which thou shalt fear, and for the sight of thine eyes which thou shalt see.

68. And the LORD shall bring thee back into Egypt in ships, by the way whereof I said unto thee: Thou shalt see it no more again; and there ye shall sell yourselves unto your enemies for bondmen and for bondwoman, and no man shall buy you.

69. These are the words of the covenant which the LORD commanded Moses to make with the children of Israel in the land of Moab, beside the covenant which He made with them in Horeb.

Chapter 29

1. And Moses called unto all Israel, and said unto them: Ye have seen all that the LORD did before your eyes in the land of Egypt unto Pharaoh, and unto all his servants, and unto all his land;

2. The great trials which thine eyes saw, the signs and those great wonders;

3. But the LORD hath not given you a heart to know, and eyes to see, and ears to hear, unto this day.

4. And I have led you forty years in the wilderness; your clothes are not waxen old upon you, and thy shoe is not waxen old upon thy foot.

5. Ye have not eaten bread, neither have ye drunk wine or strong drink; that ye might know that I am the LORD your God.

6. And when ye came unto this place, Sihon the king of Heshbon, and Og the king of Bashan, came out against us unto battle, and we smote them.

7. And we took their land, and gave it for an inheritance unto the Reubenites, and to the Gadites, and to the half-tribe of the Manassites.

8. Observe therefore the words of this covenant, and do them, that ye may make all that ye do to prosper.

Nitzavim

9. Ye are standing this day all of you before the LORD your God: your heads, your tribes, your elders, and your officers, even all the men of Israel,

10. Your little ones, your wives, and thy stranger that is in the midst of thy camp, from the hewer of thy wood unto the drawer of thy water;

11. That thou shouldest enter into the covenant of the LORD thy God-and into His oath-which the LORD thy God maketh with thee this day;

12. That He may establish thee this day unto Himself for a people, and that He may be unto thee a God, as He spoke unto thee, and as He swore unto thy fathers, to Abraham, to Isaac, and to Jacob.

13. Neither with you only do I make this covenant and this oath;

14. But with him that standeth here with us this day before the LORD our God, and also with him that is not here with us this day.

15. For ye know how we dwelt in the land of Egypt; and how we came through the midst of the nations through which ye passed;

16. And ye have seen their detestable things, and their idols, wood and stone, silver and gold, which were with them.

17. Lest there should be among you man, or woman, or family, or tribe, whose heart turneth away this day from the LORD our God, to go to serve the gods of those nations; lest there should be among you a root that beareth gall and wormwood;

18. And it come to pass, when he heareth the words of this curse, that he bless himself in his heart, saying: I shall have peace, though I walk in the stubbornness of my heart-that the watered be swept away with the dry;

19. The LORD will not be willing to pardon him, but then the anger of the LORD and His jealousy shall be kindled against that man, and all the curse that is written in this book shall lie upon him, and the LORD shall blot out his name from under heaven;

20. And the LORD shall separate him unto evil out of all the tribes of Israel, according to all the curses of the covenant that is written in this book of the law.

21. And the generation to come, your children that shall rise up after you, and the foreigner that shall come from a far land, shall say, when they see the plagues of that land, and the sicknesses wherewith the LORD hath made it sick;

22. And that the whole land thereof is brimstone, and salt, and a burning, that it is not sown, nor beareth, nor any grass growth therein, like the overthrow of Sodom and Gomorrah, Admah and Zeboiim, which the LORD overthrew in His anger, and in His wrath;

23. Even all the nations shall say Wherefore hath the LORD done thus unto this land? what meaneth the heat of this great anger?

24. Then men shall say: Because they forsook the

covenant of the LORD, the God of their fathers, which He made with them when He brought them forth out of the land of Egypt;

25. And went and served other gods, and worshipped them, gods that they knew not, and that He had not allotted unto them;

26. Therefore, the anger of the LORD was kindled against this land, to bring upon it all the curse that is written in this book;

27. And the LORD rooted them out of their land in anger, and in wrath, and in great indignation, and cast them into another land, as it is this day.

28. The secret things belong unto the LORD our God; but the things that are revealed belong unto us and to our children for ever, that we may do all the words of this law.

Chapter 30

1. And it shall come to pass, when all these things are come upon thee, the blessing and the curse, which I have set before thee, and thou shalt bethink thyself among all the nations, whither the LORD thy God hath driven thee,

2. And shalt return unto the LORD thy God, and hearken to His voice according to all that I command thee this day, thou and thy children, with all thy heart, and with all thy soul;

3. That then the LORD thy God will turn thy captivity, and have compassion upon thee, and will return and gather thee from all the peoples, whither the LORD thy God hath scattered thee.

4. If any of thine that are dispersed be in the uttermost parts of heaven, from thence will the LORD thy God gather thee, and from thence will He fetch thee.

5. And the LORD thy God will bring thee into the land which thy fathers possessed, and thou shalt possess it; and He will do thee good, and multiply thee above thy fathers.

6. And the LORD thy God will circumcise thy heart, and the heart of thy seed, to love the LORD thy God with all thy heart, and with all thy soul, that thou mayest live.

7. And the LORD thy God will put all these curses upon thine enemies, and on them that hate thee, that persecuted thee.

8. And thou shalt return and hearken to the voice of the LORD, and do all His commandments which I command thee this day.

9. And the LORD thy God will make thee over-abundant in all the work of thy hand, in the fruit of thy body, and in the fruit of thy cattle, and in the fruit of thy land, for good; for the LORD will again rejoice over thee for good, as He rejoiced over thy fathers;

10. If thou shalt hearken to the voice of the LORD thy God, to keep His commandments and His statutes which are written in this book of the law; if thou turn unto the LORD thy God with all thy heart, and with all thy soul.

11. For this commandment which I command thee this day, it is not too hard for thee, neither is it far off.

12. It is not in heaven, that thou shouldest say: Who shall go up for us to heaven, and bring it unto us, and make us to hear it, that we may do it?

13. Neither is it beyond the sea, that thou shouldest say: Who shall go over the sea for us, and bring it unto us, and make us to hear it, that we may do it?

14. But the word is very nigh unto thee, in thy mouth, and in thy heart, that thou mayest do it.

15. See, I have set before thee this day life and good, and death and evil,

16. In that I command thee this day to love the LORD thy God, to walk in His ways, and to keep His commandments and His statutes and His ordinances; then thou shalt live and multiply, and the LORD thy God shall bless thee in the land whither thou goest in to possess it.

17. But if thy heart turn away, and thou wilt not hear, but shalt be drawn away, and worship other gods, and serve them;

18. I declare unto you this day, that ye shall surely perish; ye shall not prolong your days upon the land, whither thou passest over the Jordan to go in to possess it.

19. I call heaven and earth to witness against you this day, that I have set before thee life and death, the blessing and the curse; therefore choose life, that thou mayest live, thou and thy seed;

20. To love the LORD thy God, to hearken to His voice, and to cleave unto Him; for that is thy life, and the length of thy days; that thou mayest dwell in the land which the LORD swore unto thy fathers, to Abraham, to Isaac, and to Jacob, to give them.

Vayeilech

Chapter 31

1. And Moses went and spoke these words unto all Israel.

2. And he said unto them: I am a hundred and twenty years old this day; I can no more go out and come in; and the LORD hath said unto me: Thou shalt not go over this Jordan.

3. The LORD thy God, He will go over before thee; He will destroy these nations from before thee, and thou shalt dispossess them; and Joshua, he shall go over before thee, as the LORD hath spoken.

4. And the LORD will do unto them as He did to Sihon and to Og, the kings of the Amorites, and unto their land; whom He destroyed.

5. And the LORD will deliver them up before you, and ye shall do unto them according unto all the commandment which I have commanded you.

6. Be strong and of good courage, fear not, nor be affrighted at them; for the LORD thy God, He it is that doth go with thee; He will not fail thee, nor forsake thee.

7. And Moses called unto Joshua, and said unto him in the sight of all Israel: Be strong and of good courage; for thou shalt go with this people into the land which the LORD hath sworn unto their fathers to give them; and thou shalt cause them to inherit it.

8. And the LORD, He it is that doth go before thee; He will be with thee, He will not fail thee, neither forsake thee; fear not, neither be dismayed.

9. And Moses wrote this law, and delivered it unto the priests the sons of Levi, that bore the ark of the covenant of the LORD, and unto all the elders of Israel.

10. And Moses commanded them, saying: At the end of every seven years, in the set time of the year of release, in the feast of tabernacles,

11. When all Israel is come to appear before the LORD thy God in the place which He shall choose, thou shalt read this law before all Israel in their hearing.

12. Assemble the people, the men and the women and the little ones, and thy stranger that is within thy gates, that they may hear, and that they may learn, and fear the LORD your God, and observe to do all the words of this law;

13. And that their children, who have not known, may hear, and learn to fear the LORD your God, as long as ye live in the land whither ye go over the Jordan to possess it.

14. And the LORD said unto Moses: Behold, thy days

approach that thou must die; call Joshua, and present yourselves in the tent of meeting, that I may give him a charge. And Moses and Joshua went, and presented themselves in the tent of meeting.

15. And the LORD appeared in the Tent in a pillar of cloud; and the pillar of cloud stood over the door of the Tent.

16. And the LORD said unto Moses: Behold, thou art about to sleep with thy fathers; and this people will rise up, and go astray after the foreign gods of the land, whither they go to be among them, and will forsake Me, and break My covenant which I have made with them.

17. Then My anger shall be kindled against them in that day, and I will forsake them, and I will hide My face from them, and they shall be devoured, and many evils and troubles shall come upon them; so that they will say in that day: Are not these evils come upon us because our God is not among us?

18. And I will surely hide My face in that day for all the evil which they shall have wrought, in that they are turned unto other gods.

19. Now therefore write ye this song for you, and teach thou it the children of Israel; put it in their mouths, that this song may be a witness for Me against the children of Israel.

20. For when I shall have brought them into the land which I swore unto their fathers, flowing with milk and honey; and they shall have eaten their fill, and waxen fat; and turned unto other gods, and served them, and despised Me, and broken My covenant;

21. Then it shall come to pass, when many evils and troubles are come upon them, that this song shall testify before them as a witness; for it shall not be forgotten out of the mouths of their seed; for I know their imagination how they do even now, before I have brought them into the land which I swore.

22. So, Moses wrote this song the same day, and taught it the children of Israel.

23. And he gave Joshua the son of Nun a charge, and said: Be strong and of good courage; for thou shalt bring the children of Israel into the land which I swore unto them; and I will be with thee.

24. And it came to pass, when Moses had made an end of writing the words of this law in a book, until they were finished,

25. That Moses commanded the Levites, that bore the ark of the covenant of the LORD, saying:

26. Take this book of the law, and put it by the side of the ark of the covenant of the LORD your God, that it may be there for a witness against thee.

27. For I know thy rebellion, and thy stiff neck; behold, while I am yet alive with you this day, ye have been rebellious against the LORD; and how much more after my death?

28. Assemble unto me all the elders of your tribes, and your officers, that I may speak these words in their ears, and call heaven and earth to witness against them.

29. For I know that after my death ye will in any wise deal corruptly, and turn aside from the way which I have commanded you; and evil will befall you in the end of days; because ye will do that which is evil in the sight of the LORD, to provoke Him through the work of your hands.

30. And Moses spoke in the ears of all the assembly of Israel the words of this song, until they were finished:

Ha'Azinu

Chapter 32

1. Give ear, ye heavens, and I will speak; And let the earth hear the words of my mouth.

2. My doctrine shall drop as the rain; My speech shall distil as the dew; As the small rain upon the tender grass, And as the showers upon the herb.

3. For I will proclaim the name of the LORD; Ascribe ye greatness unto our God.

4. The Rock, His work is perfect; For all His ways are justice; A God of faithfulness and without iniquity, Just and right is He.

5. Is corruption His? No; His children's is the blemish; A generation crooked and perverse.

6. Do ye thus requite the LORD, O foolish people and unwise? Is not He thy father that hath gotten thee? Hath He not made thee, and established thee?

7. Remember the days of old, Consider the years of many generations; Ask thy father, and he will declare unto thee; Thine elders, and they will tell thee.

8. When the Most High gave to the nations their inheritance, when He separated the children of men, He set the borders of the peoples according to the number of the children of Israel.

9. For the portion of the LORD is His people, Jacob the lot of His inheritance.

10. He found him in a desert land, and in the waste, a howling wilderness; He compassed him about, He cared for him, He kept him as the apple of His eye.

11. As an eagle that stirreth up her nest, Hovereth over her young, Spreadeth abroad her wings, taketh them, Beareth them on her pinions.

12. The LORD alone did lead him; And there was no strange god with Him.

13. He made him ride on the high places of the earth; And he did eat the fruitage of the field; And He made him to suck honey out of the crag, And oil out of the flinty rock;

14. Curd of kine, and milk of sheep, With fat of lambs, And rams of the breed of Bashan, and he-goats, With the kidney-fat of wheat; And of the blood of the grape, thou drankest foaming wine.

15. But Jeshurun waxed fat, and kicked - Thou didst wax fat, thou didst grow thick, thou didst become gross - And he forsook God who made him; And contemned the Rock of his salvation.

16. They roused Him to jealousy with strange gods; With abominations did they provoke Him.

17. They sacrificed unto demons, no-gods, Gods that they knew not; New gods that came up of late; Which your fathers dreaded not.

18. Of the Rock that begot thee thou wast unmindful; And didst forget God that bore thee.

19. And the LORD saw, and spurned, Because of the provoking of His sons and His daughters.

20. And He said: I will hide My face from them, I will see what their end shall be; For they are a very froward generation, Children in whom is no faithfulness.

21. They have roused Me to jealousy with a no-god; They have provoked Me with their vanities; And I will rouse them to jealousy with a no-people; I will provoke them with a vile nation.

22. For a fire is kindled in My nostril, And burneth unto the depths of the nether-world, And devoureth the earth with her produce, And setteth ablaze the foundations of the mountains.

23. I will heap evils upon them; I will spend Mine arrows upon them;

24. The wasting of hunger, and the devouring of the fiery bolt; And bitter destruction; And the teeth of beasts will I send upon them, With the venom of crawling things of the dust.

25. Without shall the sword bereave; And in the chamber's terror; Slaying both young man and virgin,

26. The suckling with the man of gray hairs.

I thought I would make an end of them; I would make their memory cease from among men;

27. Were it not that I dreaded the enemy's provocation; Lest their adversaries should misdeem; Lest they should say: Our hand is exalted; And not the LORD hath wrought all this.

28. For they are a nation void of counsel; And there is no understanding in them.

29. If they were wise, they would understand this; They would discern their latter end.

30. How should one chase a thousand; And two put ten thousand to flight; Except their Rock had given them over And the LORD had delivered them up?

31. For their rock is not as our Rock; Even our enemies themselves being judges.

32. For their vine is of the vine of Sodom; And of the fields of Gomorrah; Their grapes are grapes of gall; Their clusters are bitter;

33. Their wine is the venom of serpents, And the cruel poison of asps.

34. Is not this laid up in store with Me, Sealed up in My treasuries?

35. Vengeance is Mine, and recompense, Against the time when their foot shall slip; For the day of their calamity is at hand, And the things that are to come upon them shall make haste.

36. For the LORD will judge His people; And repent Himself for His servants; When He seeth that their stay is gone; And there is none remaining, shut up or left at large.

37. And it is said: Where are their gods, The rock in whom they trusted;

38. Who did eat the fat of their sacrifices, and drank the wine of their drink-offering? Let him rise up and help you; Let him be your protection.

39. See now that I, even I, am He; And there is no god with Me; I kill, and I make alive; I have wounded, and I heal; And there is none that can deliver out of My hand.

40. For I lift up My hand to heaven; And say: As I live for ever,

41. If I whet My glittering sword, And My hand take hold on judgment; I will render vengeance to Mine adversaries; And will recompense them that hate Me.

42. I will make Mine arrows drunk with blood, And My sword shall devour flesh; With the blood of the slain and the captives, From the long-haired heads of the enemy.

43. Sing aloud, O ye nations, of His people; For He doth avenge the blood of His servants; And doth render vengeance to His adversaries; And doth make expiation for the land of His people.

44. And Moses came and spoke all the words of this song in the ears of the people, he, and Hoshea the son of Nun.

45. And when Moses made an end of speaking all these words to all Israel,

46. He said unto them: Set your heart unto all the words wherewith I testify against you this day; that ye may charge your children therewith to observe to do all the words of this law.

47. For it is no vain thing for you; because it is your life, and through this thing ye shall prolong your days upon the land, whither ye go over the Jordan to possess it.

48. And the LORD spoke unto Moses that selfsame day, saying:

49. Get thee up into this mountain of Abarim, unto mount Nebo, which is in the land of Moab, that is over against Jericho; and behold the land of Canaan, which I give unto the children of Israel for a possession;

50. And die in the mount whither thou goest up, and be gathered unto thy people; as Aaron thy brother died in mount Hor, and was gathered unto his people.

51. Because ye trespassed against Me in the midst of the children of Israel at the waters of Meribath-kadesh, in the wilderness of Zin; because ye sanctified Me not in the midst of the children of Israel.

52. For thou shalt see the land afar off; but thou shalt not go thither into the land which I give the children of Israel.

V'Zot HaBerachah

Chapter 33

1. And this is the blessing wherewith Moses the man of God blessed the children of Israel before his death.

2. And he said: The LORD came from Sinai; And rose from Seir unto them; He shined forth from mount Paran, And He came from the myriads holy, At His right hand was a fiery law unto them.

3. Yea, He loveth the peoples, All His holy ones-they are in Thy hand; And they sit down at Thy feet, Receiving of Thy words.

4. Moses commanded us a law, An inheritance of the congregation of Jacob.

5. And there was a king in Jeshurun, When the heads of the people were gathered, All the tribes of Israel together.

6. Let Reuben live, and not die in that his men become few.

7. And this for Judah, and he said: Hear, LORD, the voice of Judah; And bring him in unto his people; His hands shall contend for him, And Thou shalt be a help against his adversaries.

8. And of Levi he said: Thy Thummim and Thy Urim be with Thy holy one, Whom Thou didst prove at Massah; With whom Thou didst strive at the waters of Meribah;

9. Who said of his father, and of his mother: I have

not seen him; Neither did he acknowledge his brethren; Nor knew he his own children; For they have observed Thy word; And keep Thy covenant.

10. They shall teach Jacob Thine ordinances, And Israel Thy law; They shall put incense before Thee; And whole burnt-offering upon Thine altar.

11. Bless, LORD, his substance; And accept the work of his hands; Smite through the loins of them that rise up against him; And of them that hate him, that they rise not again.

12. Of Benjamin he said: The beloved of the LORD shall dwell in safety by Him; He covereth him all the day, And He dwelleth between his shoulders.

13. And of Joseph he said: Blessed of the LORD be his land; For the precious things of heaven, for the dew, And for the deep that coucheth beneath,

14. And for the precious things of the fruits of the sun, And for the precious things of the yield of the moons,

15. And for the tops of the ancient mountains, And for the precious things of the everlasting hills,

16. And for the precious things of the earth and the fulness thereof, And the good will of Him that dwelt in the bush; Let the blessing come upon the head of Joseph; And upon the crown of the head of him that is prince among his brethren.

17. His firstling bullock, majesty is his; And his horns are the horns of the wild-ox; With them he shall gore the peoples all of them, even the ends of the earth; And they are the ten thousands of Ephraim, And they are the thousands of Manasseh.

18. And of Zebulun he said: Rejoice, Zebulun, in thy going out, And, Issachar, in thy tents.

19. They shall call peoples unto the mountain; There shall they offer sacrifices of righteousness; For they shall suck the abundance of the seas, And the hidden treasures of the sand.

20. And of Gad he said: Blessed be He that enlargeth Gad; He dwelleth as a lioness, And teareth the arm, yea, the crown of the head.

21. And he chose a first part for himself, For there a portion of a ruler was reserved; And there came the heads of the people, He executed the righteousness of the LORD, And His ordinances with Israel.

22. And of Dan he said: Dan is a lion's whelp, That leapeth forth from Bashan.

23. And of Naphtali he said: O Naphtali, satisfied with favour; And full with the blessing of the LORD: Possess thou the sea and the south.

24. And of Asher he said: Blessed be Asher above sons; Let him be the favoured of his brethren, And let him dip his foot in oil.

25. Iron and brass shall be thy bars; And as thy days, so shall thy strength be.

26. There is none like unto God, O Jeshurun, Who rideth upon the heaven as thy help, And in His excellency on the skies.

27. The eternal God is a dwelling-place; And underneath are the everlasting arms; And He thrust out the enemy from before thee; And said: **Destroy**.

28. And Israel dwelleth in safety; The fountain of Jacob alone; In a land of corn and wine; Yea, his heavens drop down dew.

29. Happy art thou, O Israel, who is like unto thee? A people saved by the LORD; The shield of thy help; And that is the sword of thy excellency! And thine enemies shall dwindle away before thee; And thou shalt tread upon their high places.

Chapter 34

1. And Moses went up from the plains of Moab unto mount Nebo, to the top of Pisgah, that is over against Jericho. And the LORD showed him all the land, even Gilead as far as Dan;

2. And all Naphtali, and the land of Ephraim and Manasseh, and all the land of Judah as far as the hinder sea;

3. And the South, and the Plain, even the valley of Jericho the city of palm-trees, as far as Zoar.

4. And the LORD said unto him: This is the land which I swore unto Abraham, unto Isaac, and unto Jacob, saying: I will give it unto thy seed; I have caused thee to see it with thine eyes, but thou shalt not go over thither.

5. So, Moses the servant of the LORD died there in the land of Moab, according to the word of the LORD.

6. And he was buried in the valley in the land of Moab

over against Beth-peor; and no man knoweth of his sepulchre unto this day.

7. And Moses was a hundred and twenty years old when he died: his eye was not dim, nor his natural force abated.

8. And the children of Israel wept for Moses in the plains of Moab thirty days; so, the days of weeping in the mourning for Moses were ended.

9. And Joshua the son of Nun was full of the spirit of wisdom; for Moses had laid his hands upon him; and the children of Israel hearkened unto him, and did as the LORD commanded Moses.

10. And there hath not arisen a prophet since in Israel like unto Moses, whom the LORD knew face to face;

11. In all the signs and the wonders, which the LORD sent him to do in the land of Egypt, to Pharaoh, and to all his servants, and to all his land;

12. And in all the mighty hand, and in all the great terror, which Moses wrought in the sight of all Israel.